A LOOK INSIDE THE PLAYBOOK

How Marxists Plan to Destroy America

Dr. Anthony Napoleon, Ph.D.
Yevgeni Yevtushenkov

Graphics and video in this book are part of the public domain and are used solely for their educational and illustrative value.

"A Look Inside the Playbook: How Marxists Plan to Destroy America," by Dr. Anthony Napoleon, Ph.D. and Yevgeni Yevtushenkov. ISBN: 978-1-62137-304-9 (softcover); 978-1-62137-305-6 (ebook).

Library of Congress Control Number: 2013910380

Manufactured in the United States of America

DEDICATION

Ваша основателей дал вам стране стоит экономить.

TABLE OF CONTENTS

Foreword   i

Introduction   iii

CHAPTER I- We Are Not Marxists, Communists, or Socialists   1

CHAPTER II- Know Thine Enemy   2

CHAPTER III- Circumvent Their Defenses   3

CHAPTER IV- The Enemy of My Enemy is Our Friend   4

CHAPTER V- Right and Wrong are ONLY Frames of Reference   7

CHAPTER VI- Equilibrium in All Things   9

CHAPTER VII- Tabula Rasa   11

CHAPTER VIII- Entitlement   13

CHAPTER IX- Envy and Jealousy   15

CHAPTER X- Weaken Their Borders   17

CHAPTER XI- Multiculturalism Mandate   19

CHAPTER XII- Tolerance   21

CHAPTER XIII- Verboten!   24

CHAPTER XIV- Zero Sum Economics   27

CHAPTER XV- It Takes a Village   29

CHAPTER XVI- Libertines   31

CHAPTER XVII- Slavery is Our Friend   33

CHAPTER XVIII- Inconceivable   37

CHAPTER XIX- Drugs   40

CHAPTER XX- Gun Control and Confiscation   43

CHAPTER XXI- Non Verbal Communication   46

CHAPTER XXII- Questions and Answers   55

CHAPTER XXIII- Survival Guide   61

CHAPTER XXIV- The Elites   66

CHAPTER XXV- Summary: Everything We Do Fits   69

CHAPTER XXVI- Epilogue   76

Index   120

FOREWORD

It has been a little over a half century since our movement set its sights on America. Over those 50 years we have become more sophisticated in our efforts and we have learned from our mistakes. We have been richly rewarded for our patience and methodical approach to subverting our enemy. As we begin the last leg of our revolution in this new millennium, many of our enemy's citizens have been converted into our agents and operatives.

We have transformed America's press into agencies that would put to shame our Izvestia and Pravda of our golden years back in the USSR. Our enemy's children have been "turned" and now represent one of our core demographics. We have successfully fractured America into competing groups; each estranged from the country that is their home.

Our once powerful enemy is unsure and insecure about its history and traditions. We have inculcated shame and promoted ignorance into America's children such that by the time they become adults they are ashamed of their country while having little or no insight or knowledge about the ways of the world. And they don't even know what has happened to them.

Although we have made great strides, much work needs to be done. This operations manual was designed to provide our new comrades everything they need to continue the subversion and eventual takeover of America. Our long time comrades can also benefit and stay abreast of our latest strategies and tactics by studying this manual. If you follow the principles in this operations manual you will live to see The United Socialist States of America.

INTRODUCTION

This Operations Manual is a compendium of every tool you will need to transform America into our country, a country devoid of the social injustice that has characterized it since its inglorious beginning.

As with everything we do and say we shall package our thoughts and deeds into bite sized doses of fairness, goodness, equality and justice, for who can stand against or dare criticize goodness, equality and justice?

We will begin our journey by stating our fundamental principles of action. Each chapter will give voice to a building block of our revolution. Stay true to our fundamental principles and it is only a matter of time before we can lay claim to the spoils of our victory, The United States of America.

What follows is a statement from one of our movement's defectors, a traitor by the name of Yuri Bezmenov. Despite the fact that "Yuri the Traitor" intended his statement to "wake up" our enemy, we are not worried because our movement has been so good at dumbing-down our enemy's citizens, regardless of what they hear or learn, just as Yuri "the traitor" said, they will not have the presence of mind to do anything about it.

YURI BEZMENOV EXPLAINS THE FOCUS OF THE KGB

Visit http://tinyurl.com/kgbfocus to watch.

CHAPTER I
We Are Not Marxists, Communists or Socialists

From this moment forward we are no longer Marxists, Communists, Collectivists or Socialists. We are Progressives or simply Liberals. After all, to not be Progressive is to be regressive and that is what our enemies are: Regressive and backward.

From this moment forward we shall not look or behave like those who came before us. Our grandfathers and mothers made the mistake of identifying themselves honestly in all manner and style.

You will come to trust the fact that we can hide in plain view. We have spent decades blurring the difference between image and substance. You can count on our victim's inability to see past our facade. Be filled with joy, fellow comrade, with the confidence that comes from knowing that you can hide in plain sight!

CHAPTER II
Know Thine Enemy

Our enemy conceived of, fought for and developed The United States of America. Our enemy's country was originally comprised of mostly Anglo-Christians who promulgated their values and religious doctrine through their public schools, government institutions and nuclear families. Their documents, including The Declaration of Independence, Constitution and its Bill of Rights, along with their reliance upon Biblical principles, represent a lethal threat to our existence and success of our movement.

Our enemy used to be very good at passing on to future generations their values, American principles and national identity. They were so good at handing down their values that our enemy became complacent, believing that what they put in place would always be there. We shall rely upon and exploit their complacency.

CHAPTER III
Circumvent Their Defenses

We begin as we always begin, with great patience and a plan. We must first attack our enemy's nuclear family structure because that is the framework within which they pass down their traditional American values to their children and all future generations.

We will focus our assault upon their children while they are away at school. Young minds are malleable and vulnerable. We will have access to their children for six or more hours per day, nine or more months out of the year. America's public schools will become our indoctrination camps where child by child, mind by mind, we will chip away at everything our enemy holds dear. We will not move too quickly, for it is much easier to sneak up on your enemy and kill him little by little than it is to attack everything he stands for all at once.

CHAPTER IV
The Enemy of My Enemy is Our Friend

Anglo-European Christians founded our enemy's country. Their descendants and their converts represent a serious threat to the success of our revolution.

Deists are a threat because of the following simple precept of human behavior. *When citizens believe that their rights come from God or a higher power and not from the state, they are harder to control, regulate and resist becoming members of the collective.* In place of the state, they favor a relationship with their God and their nuclear family. While we have identified Christians as our mortal enemy, we are not the only group who finds these American believers, their descendants and converts to be the enemy. Competing religions along with agnostics and atheists are our natural allies in our efforts to win the revolution. One group is particularly well suited to be our ally.

Billions of human beings are Muslim. Islam is not only a religion but it is equally, if not more so, a political movement that is dedicated to converting the world to Islam. Over the past decade our American adversaries have foolishly enraged hundreds of millions of Muslims everywhere. This has provided our revolution a point of leverage and a ready-made ally. Our political scientists have concluded that it will be much easier to overcome the forces of Islam than it will be to overcome the forces of American/Western deists. Therefore, we should promote the ascendency of Islam.

We have embarked upon a systematic devaluation of Christianity while simultaneously promoting Islam. Our efforts in this regard mean that we shall never miss an opportunity to make fun of, criticize, exclude and otherwise ridicule Christians and Christianity. Our comrades, along with avowed and unwitting sympathizers in the mass media and the entertainment industry, have been brilliant at aiding and abetting our plan. On any given day in America you can see our handiwork as Muslims, agnostics, atheists, homosexual coalitions and secular humanists ridicule Christians and Christianity, all the while promoting our religion, The Religion of Tolerance.

We shall never miss an opportunity to force Americans to permit Muslims to impose their rule of law. We are particularly interested in empowering imperialistic Muslims who are intent upon establishing a new Islamic caliphate while simultaneously infiltrating America's institutions. For example, whenever the enemy of our enemy makes efforts to introduce Shari'a law into America, we shall promote and finance these efforts, including going to court on their behalf.

Here is a representative example of our efforts at work. The enemy of our enemy has made clear their desire to erect a Mosque on the site of the destroyed 9/11 World Trade Center Towers. We support this effort and we expect our operatives and sympathizers to stop those patriotic Americans who are dedicated to preventing what they call the building of an Islamic "victory mosque" that would add "insult to injury."

Our sympathizers have taken the lead in our efforts to devalue Christianity and promote Islam. Their efforts are proof positive of the effectiveness of two of our other psychological operations: Mandated multiculturalism and the promotion of secular humanism.

We have managed to confuse and blur one of our enemy's central principles, what they call "freedom of religion." Factually, the Anglo-Christians who founded America were intent upon preventing any future government from establishing a state run/sanctioned religion, e.g., The Church of England. We have been remarkably successful at redefining this principle to mean that America cannot be true to or celebrate its deist roots. Our efforts have resulted in our ability to force Christians to rebuke their holidays, practices, celebrations and expressions of their philosophy, all the while quietly promoting the introduction of competing religions to be taught to public school children. The proponents and followers of these competing religions and philosophies are jingoistic and are not tolerant of their host country's culture or religion. We do not insist upon tolerance when it comes to the groups who compete with our enemy.

Once we have weakened Christianity to the point where we can assume control of the government, we shall begin the systematic destruction of Mosques, Churches and other threatening religious edifices, just as we did in the USSR. We will systematically destroy Islam and all but a few religions that are simpatico with or not a threat to our movement. In a short time we shall manufacture a generation of new Americans who have awakened from their religious stupor and become rock-ribbed secular humanists.

CHAPTER V
Right & Wrong are ONLY Frames of Reference

Our enemy, the United States of America, was built upon "immutable" principles, supposedly sourced from God. Our enemy uses words like "truth" and "right" and "wrong." But we have an antidote to this poison: Moral relativism.

We shall exploit man's tendency to think of himself as God, to want to be God-like, all the while we firmly insist that God does not exist. We shall exploit the inevitable conflicts that come from carnal desire governed by morality by promoting carnal desire and redefining moral principles as only points of reference. Our comrades in the media-entertainment complex have been our most important allies when it comes to achieving this goal.

The immature, pampered and narcissistic mind loves the idea that it creates reality, that man's wants, wishes and desires are more important than and take precedence over countries, documents, parents or yes, even God.

The younger we begin the cleansing of our enemy's children's conscience the better and more complete will be the final result. Years ago our behavioral experts identified the need to excise prayer from public schools. Removing prayer in these government run institutions has been one of our greatest successes. Still, we should remain vigilant because our enemy is intent upon undoing our social engineering successes. Our enemy has proposed a "moment of silence" approach to circumventing our ban on public school prayer. The mere act of a moment of silence or spiritual reflection serves as a meta-communication that there is a higher power than man, that man is not the end all, be all. If the dominant religious philosophy is Christianity then a moment of reflection inevitably encourages the imagination to conjure up Christian images.

We should never lose sight of the fact that the void created by our excision of religion in America's culture must be filled with something. We intend to fill the void with a blind allegiance to the state, to the collective and to the village. We shall encourage man to become a slavish devotee to the "Green religion." Holidays rooted in the change of the seasons, health foods and new age-psychology are not a threat to our movement and are consistent with our revolutionary goals.

CHAPTER VI
Equilibrium in All Things

No two things, people, cultures or events are equal. While we must never forget this fact, our enemy must never be allowed to know this fact. We must convince our enemy that all things should be equal in every way, and if they are not, it is because of the social injustice of our enemy and his country. If our enemy dares to suggest that two things are different, with one being better than the other, we should immediately label that person as intolerant. By attaching the suffix "phobe" to any group sympathetic or helpful to our cause we can stifle reasoned discourse, e.g., "Islamophobe." By adding the suffix "er" to any word that poses a threat we can diminish it, e.g., "birth-er" or "hate-er."

When we convince our enemy's citizens of the truth of the equilibrium distortion they will be unable to discriminate, as in telling two or more things apart. If they cannot discriminate, they will be unable to separate that which will kill them from that will protect them.

We shall promote and sponsor laws that would forbid law enforcement agencies from identifying suspects by their gender, race, age, height or weight. When we pass these laws we will have completely hobbled our enemy and that means the time will be near to make our big move.

Our enemy prides itself on promoting equal opportunity. We pride ourselves on equal outcomes. Our position is quite simple; any person who does not have what another person has is a victim of social injustice. Remember, we must never miss an opportunity to accuse our enemy of engaging in social injustice.

CHAPTER VII
Tabula Rasa

TSUNG TSUNG, AGE 4, PLAYS HAYDN ON THE PIANO

Visit http://tinyurl.com/tsungplays to watch.

You must assert and enforce the principle of man being born as a blank slate. This is because for our movement to be successful we must convince people to explain the differences between cultures, people, religions, governments, anything you can imagine, as differences emanating from the environment and NOT from merit, talent, industry or anything that emanates from within the person. Notions such as personal responsibility and God-given talent are poison to our movement. We must condition children to believe in communal and socially rooted determinism, not personal responsibility.

Even when confronted with, as our enemy would say, "God-given talent," we shall emphasize the environment and diminish internal factors.

Rest assured that our view will come to dominate and give us the leverage needed to control our enemy. This is because citizens like to think that given the right opportunity and environment, they too would have been great, talented and rich. It feels good to blame others or outside forces for your shortcomings.

The fact that the vast majority of people are average, by definition, means we can blame our enemy for the average person's relative lack of brilliance, talent and achievement. We shall brainwash all children to be treated as though they are geniuses in the making. We shall give them rewards, accolades and special achievement awards for merely showing up in class. Remember, there are no "average" children, only brilliant children who have been oppressed by our enemy.

Never forget that our enemy has used environmental advantage in the form of legacy affirmative action and "hot-housing" of average children. When you can point to an average person who attended an Ivy League school, for example, because his father or mother attended that same school, you can inflame class warfare. Another example of applying this principle is to point out "trust fund children" and their tendency to live wasteful and miscreant lives. Remember that our enemy's elitist behavior is one of our greatest allies.

CHAPTER VIII
Entitlement

We shall condition children to expect rewards and accolades regardless of their relative performance. We shall teach the teachers to stigmatize higher achievers because those people make the lower achievers feel bad.

By enforcing the principle of equality in all things, so too shall we teach teachers to reward lack-luster performance with the same accolades as those who exhibit stellar performance.

Our enemy became powerful, in part, by rewarding merit and admiring accomplishment. We recognize and shall exploit the fact that being exceptional is, by definition, relatively rare. This situation is a breeding ground for envy.

We can cultivate guilt among the "winners" merely over the fact that they won and create envy among "losers" over merely not winning. Americans must be encouraged to feel bad about being the richest country on Earth. Our teachers must conflate "winning" with the mere fact of existing. When we achieve this, the average person will feel entitled to have everything that the most talented and hardworking people have. The principle is simple to apply, reward children for merely showing up and continually reinforce narcissistic tendencies in all people. Remember to always stress this point, ANY deficit or lack of brilliance, wealth or achievement in any person should be blamed on America's unfair economic, religious and cultural practices. We are here to remedy those inequities.

CHAPTER IX
Envy & Jealousy

After our public school's manufactured two generations of entitlement minded citizens, we took the next step and encouraged man's natural tendency to be envious and jealous. You will have an ally in man's nature, which tends to develop envy and jealousy absent a moral edict against such feelings. Since we have destroyed morality in favor of hedonism and moral relativism, we will find it very easy to promote our particular type of envy, namely, class envy.

When we point out the differences between the "haves" and the "have nots," remember we are talking to the "have nots." We will emphasize to them this fundamental principle of our revolution: **The haves MUST HAVE exploited you, the have nots, because otherwise you, too, would have what the achievers have in their life.** Once we start the ball rolling, class envy fueled by jealousy will prime the pump for our revolution's end game: confiscation and redistribution of wealth. Permit me to repeat a key point of leverage. Our enemy has among its ranks many average children whose parents were very successful. These hot-housed children were given their own brand of affirmative action called: *legacy affirmative action*. Point out these average children who live like kings and queens and have been given every social advantage imaginable. They are proof of our enemy's power over the average man. Legacy affirmative action will also serve another purpose for our revolution, the push toward affirmative action for low achievers. When we force the elevation of low achievers into positions of power and influence we demoralize those people who do possess merit and work hard but are not afforded such social engineering advantages. Low achievers in positions of power can ruin cities, states and an entire nation. Once ruined, we can move in and take it over.

CHAPTER X
Weaken Their Borders

Our enemy cannot be defeated as long as its borders and Anglo-European dominated culture remain intact. Our leaders recognized early on that one of the best ways to destroy our enemy is to encourage other less evolved cultures to infiltrate our enemy's country in the form of non-assimilating immigrants.

The key to our success is *"non-assimilating" immigrants*. We must make sure the floodgates are opened to non-assimilating immigrants by discouraging and circumventing the need for immigrants to go through the legal requirements of becoming a U.S. Citizen.

Legal immigrants, especially from non-third world countries who share our enemy's religious and philosophical ideals, are dangerous to our movement because more often than not these "new" citizens have a burning desire to become Americans. Remember, willing converts are usually the most dogmatic members of a religion. Many non-third world immigrants have a work ethic and moral fiber that are synchronous with traditional American values. These cultures emphasize merit, industry and personal responsibility. So be careful and realize that not all immigrants are created equal.

Promote illegal immigration whenever you can and you will discourage legal immigration at the same time you will flood our enemy with people who will vote for us because they will conclude we are on their side. We shall demonstrate solidarity with non-assimilating immigrants by supporting public welfare, the creation of sanctuary cities and by quietly funding and backing jingoistic movements like La Raza, Aztlan, Reconquista or Islamic immigration.

We can encourage non-assimilating immigrants to overwhelm our enemy's health care and welfare systems. As more and more third world country immigrants flood into our enemy's country they will bring with them not only their third world jingoistic cultural practices but their diseases, as well. We intend to reacquaint our enemy's health care system with once eradicated diseases while forcing existent citizens to pay for the health care of non-assimilating immigrants. Your "magic mantra" that will neutralize anyone who dares to argue that borders should be secure is this: "You are anti-immigrant, intolerant and a hater." It works EVERY TIME.

CHAPTER XI
Multiculturalism Mandate

America had at one time one dominant language, English. Our enemy had at one time a culture characterized by all things Americana, even if some parts of Americana were flavored with influences from other cultures. Our enemy's country also had a distinct Christian philosophical underpinning.

We embarked upon the great destruction of Americana in the 1960's by making American children feel bad about their country and cultural heritage. We used events of that era to fuel our movement and to demoralize Americans. We pounced on any political or economic blunder on the part of our enemy.

We continue to introduce and promote other cultural practices as equal to, if not superior to, Americana. We have denied generations of Americans pride in their unique history and identity while encouraging other cultures to jealously protect their unique identity. One outstanding example of our success is that America's children in the new millennium have little or no pride in their country. Some pockets of patriotism exist, but for the most part, we have completely subverted our enemy's children. It is now fashionable to blame America first.

We frown upon the celebration of Christmas. We not only get away with doing that, we are congratulated. We look down upon The Pledge of Allegiance or similar displays of patriotism and have, in many schools and official gatherings, eradicated any formal displays of patriotism. We make fun of all things Americana while extolling the virtues of foreign food, film, music, religion and sexual mores.

You will notice that the act of holding one's hand over one's heart during the playing of our enemy's National Anthem is no longer the rule. Look closely and you will see that within the highest echelons of our enemy's institutions, and even among its highest office holders, displays of national pride have been limited or eradicated. Our comrades have shown great courage in rejecting displays of national pride and allegiance. Watch this video and fully appreciate the courage and dedication required to make this public display. And most of all, feel confident and empowered that we were not uncovered and rousted from our lairs for this act of courage and bravery.

AN UNCOMMON ACT OF COURAGE AND DEDICATION
Visit http://tinyurl.com/uncommonact to watch.

CHAPTER XII
Tolerance

When confronted with a seemingly insurmountable problem we turn to our comrades in the behavioral sciences. We faced such a problem that is as old as man himself, man's desire to protect his national identity, culture and way of life. Our ultimate revolutionary goal has been to subvert our enemy's cultural identity, deny its people their national pride and convince them to relinquish that which made them unique within all the other cultures and peoples of the world. In service to our goals, we invented the religion of tolerance, with an emphasis upon the word "religion."

We have been successful at inculcating the religion of tolerance into the children of our enemy without thought or reflection. The modification we made to our enemy's mind created this delusion: Tolerance is the antidote to intolerance, and intolerance is always, without exception, bad. This delusion is not to be questioned, ever.

When our behavioral experts initially presented the "tolerance solution" we were skeptical. We wondered how would it be possible to convince people to tolerate that which will eventually destroy their national identity, their culture, their way of life, even them? The answer provided insight into our enemy and how people process information. The answer demonstrates our power and our brilliant psychologist consultant comrades.

Before tolerance can have its powerful effect teachers must teach that Anglo-Christian children are bad, that they are intolerant by design, their parents are intolerant and that the world is comprised of the victims of their intolerance. These lessons are taught to Anglo children simultaneously with their purported victims watching and learning. We do this in our indoctrination camps called America's public schools.

Study the photo that begins this chapter. The Muslim woman is a member of a theo-political ideology that insists upon converting the entire world to her ideology. Her male counterparts are intolerant of allowing her to show her face. Women in her culture are more often than not forbidden to drive automobiles. The members of her ideology believe without limit or reservation that all other religions, other than Islam, are heresy. Her theo-political philosophy condones female "honor killings" and often punishes homosexual behavior with death. Female Muslim children in some Islamic countries are subjected to the surgical excision of the clitoris with 85% of their vaginal opening sewn shut. Yet, if you study the picture, it is the Anglo woman and the culture she represents who is portrayed to be the intolerant person in the photo. Without bragging, when you look at that photo revel in our brilliance at reversing the roles of who is and who is not intolerant by casting the Muslim woman as the victim of intolerance by an Anglo woman.

What we have been able to do is to force our enemy to tolerate intolerance. We do not tolerate capitalism but we have been quite successful at convincing capitalists that they should tolerate our Socialist policies. We do not tolerate American exceptionalism, but we have been quite successful at convincing Americans that our ideology is vastly superior to theirs, that we are exceptional.

The cost of tolerating those cultures and people who are intolerant has been lost on our enemy because we have not permitted such a question to be asked anywhere in our enemy's educational system. If that question is broached we have instructed our teachers to immediately cry, "you're being intolerant." "You are a hater." Media elites on both ends of the political continuum have been muzzled. You'll never hear them come out and address our psychological operation because that would jeopardize their multi-million dollar paychecks.

We have elevated the concept of intolerance to the level of a religious edict that is never to be questioned. This is quite interesting given that our efforts have been successful at deleting religious imagery and values from our enemy's culture. We know that God is myth, but when necessary and when it suits our needs, we will tap into religious dogmatism and apply it in service to our revolution.

We must be wary of any counter-revolutionary force that would define tolerance of those who are intolerant as self-destructive. To protect against this the first person perspective is critically important to enforce. Tolerance is always viewed from the perspective of the intolerant Anglo-Christian. But if our enemy were to reject the first person perspective and view the issue of tolerance from the first person to the person or culture being tolerated, then we may be confronted, once again, with an insurmountable problem. For now, our teachers are becoming more and more supplicant and our enemy's culture has been turned on itself. We should never fall prey, however, to the virus we have unleashed on our enemy. **Remember, by tolerating intolerance one actually promotes intolerance.** You must know this but our enemy must **never** be allowed to even think about it.

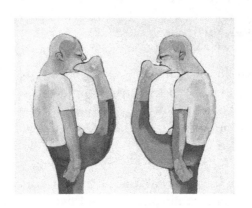

CHAPTER XIII
Verboten!

Just as we are not Marxist or Communist revolutionaries, but are now Progressives or Liberals, we cannot expect to enforce our law of Verboten by calling it that. Rather, our censorship is shrouded in a desire to be correct, sensitive and fair in what others should be allowed to say because what kind of person, after all, desires to be incorrect, insensitive or unfair? It is beautiful isn't it?

We must enforce a strict prohibition against our enemy ever speaking or writing the truth, especially about our movement or us. But how can we do this when our enemy has Constitutional protections of free speech? Easy, we brainwash Americans to believe that some speech should be unacceptable, intolerable and, dare I say, Verboten!

Our enemy has come to accept the proposition that some speech is unacceptable. For instance, our enemy's legal system states that one cannot scream "fire" in a crowded theater, unless of course there really is a fire. We, dear comrades, are the fire but our enemy does not have the stomach to scream "fire." Ironically, they are afraid to scream the truth because it may cause a stampede out of the theater. Our enemy is both weak and stupid.

Our comrades in the media-entertainment complex will flood our enemy with vapid pop-culture media that will not only occupy our enemy's consciousness but over time will dull their wit. We will know we are winning when America's public is more likely to know the name of a vapid reality TV personality than a high-ranking government official.

We must never allow Anglo-Christian truths to be spoken, especially taught. Anything that exposes who we are or what our true motives happen to be must be squelched in no uncertain terms.

For example, we have been very successful at making it socially unacceptable to use the word that defines two or more people working together to achieve a common goal. What is that word? Conspiracy! We call people who draw attention to our collective efforts "conspiracy nuts." We have so successfully stigmatized the term "conspiracy" that anyone who dares to even suggest that there may be Marxist conspirators in their government may as well self-destruct right then and there.

We forbid or frown upon the greeting Merry Christmas, but in its place we sanction Happy Holidays. We forbid use of the terms "man" or "woman" but in their place we sanction using the term "person." We have excised from acceptable lexicon any term of endearment that references a person's gender. We frown upon our enemy's children wearing clothes that depict the American flag, illustrations of its military branches or the colors of their flag. To do so is "insensitive," and as we all know, sensitivity training is a major firewall that protects us from our enemies.

Our enemy is forbidden to speak of what it terms American exceptionalism. On the other hand, we not only sanction, we reward those who speak of America's imperialism. Dare to say anything pejorative about any religious or political group critical of America and we shall be quick to squelch that speech. On the other hand, we encourage derogatory speech directed at all things Americana; including works of art, comedy sketches, books or movies. We strongly encourage speech that makes fun of or criticizes Christianity; especially Anglo-European rooted Christianity. If our enemy dares to speak the truth we demand an apology or genuflection to our control.

CHAPTER XIV
Zero Sum Economics

Whenever we talk about economic injustice what we are really saying is that America's economy is a zero-sum game. This means that if one man makes more money than another man it is because the richer man took money from the poorer man. Our assertion rests upon this assumption; there is only a fixed amount of money to go around. Zero-sum economics must be accepted as true if we are to convince our enemy's citizens to allow us to take control of their government in order to confiscate then redistribute wealth.

A VOTER EXPRESSES HER APPRECIATION FOR
GOVERNMENT BENEFITS

Visit http://tinyurl.com/voterexplains to watch.

Our enemy believes in this truth, invention, creativity and entrepreneurship grow the economic pie. But never fear, most people never create anything and will never understand nor accept as true an expanding pie economic model. Let's just say that the concept of the expanding economic pie requires more thought than we have allowed our enemy to possess or apply. Moreover, our economic model uses payoffs, payouts, the dole and welfare as incentives for acceding power to us. You would be surprised at how cheaply we can buy votes. Part of the attraction of our welfare-state economic model is that those who are promised government checks and benefits know that the money they receive comes from those greedy, nasty capitalists. Payback is a powerful motivator. When capitalists fight the welfare state all we have to do is frame their efforts as evidence of their selfishness to protect their already monumental wealth.

Never miss an opportunity to pit the rich against the poor. The poor man in America now believes that he deserves to have exactly what the rich man has; after all, the rich man took it from the poor man. It is only fair.

CHAPTER XV
It Takes a Village

Our enemy's nuclear family structure must be weakened and eventually dissolved. One way we will be able to accomplish this is to subvert the family in favor of community child rearing. We can subvert the power of the nuclear family by promoting laws that give children power over their parents. When parents become afraid of their own children we will know that we are well on our way to destroying our enemy.

We can weaken the nuclear family by promoting what we call "non-traditional" lifestyle families. Two mothers, two fathers or grandmothers forced to rear children should be promoted, as these family units are anathema to Christian ideals. You may wonder how we can promote such family structures? Our most persuasive argument is rooted in our "religion of tolerance" and "acceptance."

Our enemy will help us in our efforts because they will self-destruct their own nuclear family structure. How can we assist this process? We will encourage hedonism, make divorce easy, discourage having children and immerse our enemy in a culture of perversion, free sex and coed workplaces. As our plan takes hold, our enemy will self-destruct their nuclear families so that all we have to do is clean up their mess.

We can also undermine the nuclear family structure by promoting child emancipation, providing children with their own lawyers, giving female children the right to abort their children without so much as notifying their parents. Our efforts will promote what has been termed, "Village Raising."

Our Village's standards will one day trump the nuclear family's standards. We will, one day soon, make parents afraid to discipline their children lest their children call the Village enforcers to intervene. Yes, it really does, take a Village to Raise a Child, **OUR CHILD!**

MSNBC HOST DECLARES COLLECTIVE OWNERSHIP OF OUR ENEMY'S CHILDREN

Visit http://tinyurl.com/msnbcchild to watch.

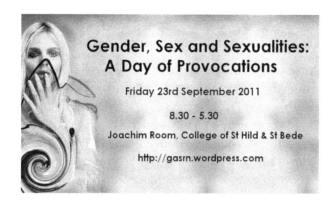

Gender, Sex and Sexualities:
A Day of Provocations

Friday 23rd September 2011

8.30 - 5.30

Joachim Room, College of St Hild & St Bede

http://gasrn.wordpress.com

CHAPTER XVI
Libertines

Little did we know that our own hedonistic pleasure seeking would one day help foment our revolution. We have come to realize that sex without obligation or procreation is central to our movement's eventual success.

When people have sex and procreate in committed relationships, as our enemy's traditional Christian teachings mandate, men and women tend to "settle down" and focus upon their family. Limited government Conservatism, the bane of our existence, is often spawned by a committed family structure. Never forget, we must insist that the secular humanist collective community is dominant to the deist's ideal of the nuclear family.

Promoting "free" sex is easy because if you can remove the guilt and responsibility from sex you encourage hedonism and hedonism promotes focus upon self, not family, church or country. Sex can lead to pregnancy, so we must make abortions guilt free, cheap and easy. We shall push for the notion that birth control pills must be paid for by the community. Never forget, parents tend to be more conservative if their focus is upon their nuclear family.

We will one day make birth control, condom and sex-toy commercials as common as ads for candy bars. When you see that, you'll know we are well on our way to destroying our enemy's family structure. Anything that blurs or weakens the traditional mother, father, children, nuclear family structure, is a boon to our eventual success. Whenever you see a movement or person whose identity and sexual practices would blur or weaken the American traditional paradigm, encourage it, promote it and, as always, justify your efforts using the mantle of equality, social justice and the "religion of tolerance."

You'll have man's innate carnal nature on your side. Our most vocal sympathizers are often unattractive libertine males within the media-entertainment complex. Since the very beginning of show business these unattractive men have benefited by adopting our "free love" mantra. It was the only way many of them could convince women to have sex with them, along with administering mind-altering substances or promising young naïve women a part in one of their movies or television shows. Our enemy is critical of this genre of sexual hedonist. America's traditional values promote guilt in this population. As we have outlined, guilt is a negative feeling and like all negative feelings, it should be eradicated with a vengeance.

CHAPTER XVII
Slavery is Our Friend

Black Americans pose a virulent threat to our movement. This is because Black Americans are the most devoutly religious racial group in America. The vast majority of Black Americans are Christian. Black Christians have traditionally been conservative and as we have warned, and it is worth repeating, conservatism is toxic to our revolution.

Our goal of fracturing our enemy's cultural identity means, in part, fracturing the relationship between Blacks and Whites. While a racial war may be theoretically possible and advantageous, we have found a much easier way to fracture America's Black and White citizens, and that is by exploiting the historical fact of slavery.

Keep in mind that we have created two generations of American children who have been brainwashed to believe that they are entitled to and should expect to be grand successes, regardless of their talent, industry, intelligence or anything else. Of course, most people are average. They will grow up to become members of the proletariat. This dynamic sets the stage for fracturing the Black family and driving a wedge between Black and White Americans. Here is how this works:

We have implanted and must continually reinforce the idea that the reason any Black person is not a multi-millionaire, brilliant, owns a beautiful big house and car, is because of oppression at the hands of the White man. In keeping with this mantra, slavery (or the White man) is the perfect excuse for the average Black American to explain why he or she never became great. Never mind that slavery ended 150 years ago or that many Black people then and now were and are very accomplished. Never mind that America's Black population comprises the most successful and accomplished Black Africans living anywhere on the planet, including Africa. These facts are irrelevant in the face of man's (Black's and White's) desperate search to explain why he or she is not as accomplished as the rich and successful people portrayed in the media. Remember, we have created children of all races who believe they are *entitled* to be great.

Moreover, we have taught and insist upon White guilt, regardless of whether or not White people living today had relatives who ever owned, condoned or benefited from slavery. We know, but must never allow others to know, that over 97% of Anglo-Americans, even in the South, never owned slaves. We can just as easily insist upon displays of debilitating guilt from a White person who had put their life on the line during the civil rights movement of the 1960's or had married a Black person or had only recently immigrated to America as we could from an abusive slave master living in the 1820's.

The guilt we have cultivated among White people will serve us well, especially if and when we find a Black leader. If we can find a Black comrade leader we will have insured that he or she can never be criticized as one of us lest we cry "racism." After two generations of promoting White guilt the mere mention of the epithet "racist" is enough to squelch any White person's credibility and shut them up immediately. White people ridden with our imposed guilt over the fact of slavery will vote in droves for our Black comrade as if that act alone will finally get rid of the guilt we have inculcated into them over the years. Still, despite all these cultural trends moving in our direction, we will have to deal with the Black Conservative.

The Black Conservative represents a potentially deadly threat to our movement, especially our plans to fracture the relationship between White and Black people. The Black Conservative, especially since he is likely to be accomplished, undermines our central thesis about the lasting effects of slavery and the innate evilness of the White man. But never fear, our comrades who are expert in human behavior science have taught us to reach into the history of slavery to find a ready-made weapon against the Black conservative. We are expert at using stigmatized labels, and one label we can use with great effectiveness is the label of "Uncle Tom."

We advise you to be careful when throwing around racially charged terms if you are non-Black. But you can suggest that a Black conservative is an "Uncle Tom" without saying it. For example, you can say: "There have always been, unfortunately and tragically, Black people who have identified with their masters to the detriment of their Black brothers and sisters." Our Black sympathizers will be quick to use the term "Uncle Tom" along with every racially pejorative term in existence. If you are a White comrade, simply sit back and allow the drama to unfold.

We can use any Black Conservative's success against him in the same way we exploit envy of successful people of all races. But with the Black Conservative we should strive to combine envy and jealousy with the "Uncle Tom" epithet. Never fail to employ tactics that serve to foment a Black stereotype while undermining the credibility of a Black Conservative. Our audience will confuse our psychological operations that promote Black stereotypes as confirmation that it is our enemy who is racist, not us. For example, one of the most effective tactics to use against virtually any Black Conservative is to expose him to be a philanderer, an adulterer or sexual libertine. It is beautiful, isn't it?

Remember, whenever we remind our Black brothers and sisters of the injustice of slavery we are promoting victimhood. Victimhood means that there is a victimizer by definition, and we shall drive home the point that the victimizer is the rich White man and the government he created for himself. Once the relationship between the races is fractured, we can more easily take over our enemy's country as his attention will be focused elsewhere and we will have a reliable voting block in the Black American perma-victim. We have nature on our side because identity politics taps into one of man's most basic instincts, the tendency to vote for someone who is a member of the same tribe, regardless of merit, qualifications or accomplishment.

Our efforts should be focused upon creating one more fracture, and that is the fracture of the Black nuclear family. By creating an underclass of Black perma-victims within the confines of "rich White America" we can destroy traditional Black families. We must encourage young Black women to behave like whores and Black men to want to be or admire pimps and embrace being absentee fathers.

We will encourage these behaviors using popular culture. We will know that our efforts are working when Black children sing songs about "pimps and ho's" in the same way their grandparents sang about love and marriage. One other benefit to promoting this behavior is that we can help to finance our revolution by raking in profits from the sale of Black oriented music, clothes and other digital media that celebrate our destruction of the Black family.

CHAPTER XVIII
Inconceivable

Sport's psychologists teach players the art of not falling prey to the "head fake." One technique that is used to prevent falling for a head fake has to do with where players focus their eyes. Players are instructed to watch the direction of their opponent's hips, not their head. Hips don't lie; heads do lie. But what happens if the change in direction of your opponent's hips is so dramatic, so out of the norm, that it becomes inconceivable that the player would or could actually move in that direction?

Once again, man's nature is one of our strongest allies. Our intent is clear; we intend to overthrow the United States of America. In its place we intend to install a Socialist regime. Before we can replace the existent government and economic system we must first destroy the solvency of the in-place economic and cultural system of America. As long as capitalism remains strong and America's culture remains

37

intact, including its dominance and respect in the world, we have little hope of overthrowing and taking control of the United States.

Our operatives and political sympathizers are smart, very well educated and dedicated revolutionaries. Their efforts are, by design, intended to destroy the economic integrity of the United States, ruin America's place of strength and respect in the world and to subvert the very Constitution to which our sympathizers and operatives in government have pledged allegiance. You may ask: **But isn't that treason? The answer is yes, of course, but treason is inconceivable, at least in America and especially when it involves one or more of their popular leaders.**

Americans accept, at least theoretically, that treason does exist. They know about it, some write about it, but virtually everyone has concluded and deeply believe that treason is something that happens to other cultures, other countries. Treason is something that may have occurred in the past, but not today, and certainly not in the United States of America.

The lesson here is that we need not be overly cautious when engaging in treasonous behaviors as long as we fly under the radar. When our government operatives promote policies and programs that have the effect of destroying the economic integrity of the country they swore to protect, Conservatives and other opponents of our revolution will attribute our agent's behavior to "failed" policies or choices that are stupid or ill-conceived. If not ill conceived or stupid, then our operatives and agents will be accused of playing politics or as believing in a political point of view that simply doesn't work. Conservatives will NEVER label our behavior as treasonous and our operatives as guilty of treason because to do so is inconceivable. The fact of the matter is our enemy has no stomach for what they would be forced to do should they identify, then confront, our treasonous behavior.

By the way, there is no reason for our government operatives to "play dumb" when we are accused of promoting policies and programs that are destructive of the country we swore to protect. Surely our enemies know that we are smart, extremely well educated, articulate and worldly. It doesn't matter; our enemy's failure to identify our motives and intent is rooted in mankind's inability to conceive of that which is inconceivable. Our enemies do not have the stomach to call out treasonous behavior even when it is right before their eyes.

CHAPTER XIX
Drugs

Our revolution benefits when our enemy's citizens are supplicant and focused upon their pleasure to the exclusion of everything else. Citizens who possess a stubborn national identity, traditional American patriots, comprise the ranks of counter-revolutionary forces and pose a dangerous threat to our movement.

Man's nature, which has been our ally up until now, works against us because we are all about control. Control is how we effectuate our revolution. Man hates to be controlled even when it is for the collective benefit of all. This is why our revolution is most likely to succeed when it manifests in incremental steps and our control remains hidden, for the most part, within a facade of fairness, equality, social justice and tolerance.

To counter man's tendency to resist control we have embarked upon altering how our enemy perceives, processes and emotionally reacts to information and circumstances. We have done this using the sophisticated psychological warfare tactics outlined in this manual, but those tactics, though powerful, are not always enough and more can be done.

When America's collective mind is biochemically made to be "mellow" and void of wariness about change (our euphemism for control), we can impose our revolution on America without fear that there will be reprisal against our agents and operatives. This is because our enemy's citizens will have neither the energy nor the motivation to do anything about the incremental changes and control we impose on them.

Our subversion of American's minds has made it normal for our enemy's citizens to react to every little change in their mental state. We want citizens who react negatively to ANY anxiety, worry, lack of energy, distraction, "blues" or any other change in their mental state that distracts from their right to carefree pleasure at all times. Furthermore, once the targets of our revolution become tuned into the slightest unpleasant changes in their mental state, we shall encourage and promote the use of pharmaceuticals to make those feelings disappear.

Our ultimate goal is to remove the stigma associated with "getting high." You will know that our efforts have succeeded when "getting high" is no longer frowned upon, and in fact, is viewed as a normal, even healthy activity.

We will de-stigmatize marijuana and stigmatize tobacco. Tobacco is a cash crop for many of our enemy's conservative states. Tobacco company executives have resisted our movement over the years and have been financiers for conservative politicians. So while we intend to make it virtually impossible to light up a cigarette anywhere in America, we can and will make smoking marijuana commonplace. Remember, when under the influence of marijuana most people simply want to relax, laugh, eat junk food and not worry about such things as the takeover of their country. SSRI-modifying prescription drugs will be promoted as a cure-all for everything from depression to OCD. We shall also promote the use of prescription psychotropic medications for use in children. By the time these medicated children become adults they will have become psychologically, if not physically, addicted to substances just to make it through the day.

Promoting drugs has another benefit to our cause other than psychologically neutering our enemy's citizens; drugs promote the displacement of responsibility. Can't focus because we are busy bombarding you with subliminal images designed to make you hate your country, take a pill. Can't find a job, because we are imploding your economy, don't worry get high or shoot up. Don't have the energy to make it in a capitalist economy, don't worry, get a prescription and vote for us, and on and on and on.

When we promote the use of drugs while simultaneously keeping them illegal, we empower and encourage drug cartels and inner-city Black and Hispanic entrepreneurs who will reject legitimate paths to material success in America. Once these groups drop out of traditional America they will dissolve the Black family, promote crime, encourage hedonism and scare our enemy into withdrawing from America's cities into the "safe" suburbs. It is within engineered inner-city ghettos that our movement can breed a seething subclass that will drain and prey upon our enemy's country. When we do take control, we will know how to deal with these people in the inner-city, after all, we've done it before.

CHAPTER XX
Gun Control & Confiscation

Earlier we quoted from traitor and ex-KGB operative, Yuri Bezmenov. Now I wish to quote from another traitor, the late Aleksander Solzhenitsyn. In his expose on mother USSR, entitled Gulag Archipelago, our former late comrade, now traitor, said this:

> *"And how we burned in the camps later, thinking: What would things have been like if every Security I operative, when he went out at night to make an arrest, had been uncertain whether he would return alive and had to say good-bye to his family? Or if, during periods of mass arrests, as for example in Leningrad, when they arrested a quarter of the entire city, people had not simply sat there in their lairs, paling with terror at every bang of the downstairs door and at every step on the staircase, but had understood they had nothing left to lose and had boldly set up in the downstairs hall an ambush of half a dozen people with axes, hammers, pokers, or whatever else was at hand?... The Organs would very quickly have suffered a shortage of officers*

and transport and, notwithstanding all of Stalin's thirst, the cursed machine would have ground to a halt! If...if...We didn't love freedom enough. And even more - we had no awareness of the real situation.... We purely and simply deserved everything that happened afterward."

Solzhenitsyn reminds us of a key element of human behavior, and that is self-preservation. The founders of our enemy's country understood all too well that an armed citizenry is the last outpost of protection against a tyrannical government. Keep in mind that our enemy's military could overcome any citizen based militia, but our experts have concluded that at this time in history, America's military and its federal agents of any stripe will have little appetite for carrying out an attack on their fellow citizens. Add to this reluctance Solzhenitsyn's point about a government agent's concern as to whether or not he will return home from his government ordered door-to-door rousting of traditional Americans, and we have a problem.

Confiscating guns from Americans, especially Americans living in the South, is not going to be easy. But never fear our human behavior experts have an answer. We shall be ever vigilant for a spontaneous attack on children or other helpless victims by someone, usually a madman, using a gun, hopefully using what has come to be known as an "assault weapon." When that event occurs, as it most certainly will in any country with over 315 million people, we will have in place and be ready to roll out gun control legislation that will limit, and one day confiscate, American's guns.

America's White liberal dense population centers have had little or no exposure to guns, thanks to our operatives in city government. Our enemy's public schools have been transformed into "Gun Free Zones." This means that our enemy's children have had very limited exposure to guns.

We have promoted fear of guns in every segment of our enemy's citizenry.

We must confront the NRA, a group of conservative gun rights Americans who have become our mortal enemy. This is a battle where we can rely upon our allies in the sympathetic media. Our media comrades have been conditioned to pounce on any gun violence event where the shooter can fit a stereotype of a *conservative* "gun nut." Conversely, our allies in the media will systematically block dissemination of any use of a gun that actually saved a life. The American voters will never seek out stories on their own about those who have survived an assault or criminal act because they possessed a firearm. Our operatives, along with our sympathizers, will make sure it won't be easy for the average American to access this information even if he wanted to learn.

While actively suppressing information about the benefits of gun ownership, we will blast the airways with any story about a shooter and his weapon that happens to kill an innocent. Keep this in mind, the younger the victim of the shooter, the more likely we will be able to use these events to one day confiscate all guns. As with all of our efforts, piece-by-piece, gun-by-gun, we will move our agenda forward until one day we have disarmed our enemy.

CHAPTER XXI
Non Verbal Communication

We are the masters of drama. We are expert at displaying symbolic outrage, dismissiveness and superiority. Our agents and sympathizers are masters at communicating the subliminal message that those who would expose us for who we really are lack credibility, are stupid, ignorant, crazy or just plain unimportant.

Our human behavior consultants have taught us that coming out and verbally demeaning and dismissing our opponents is not nearly as effective as undermining them by and through our non-verbal communication cues we display using contrived psychodrama.

We are after emotional impact, and our experts tell us and our experience informs us, that the majority of any emotional message is communicated on the non-verbal channel of communication. Since non-verbal communication is a visual element, words describing how it is done are not quite as effective as showing you what dismissive and superiority non-verbal communication looks like.

What follows are examples of our operatives and/or sympathizers using non-verbal communication to undermine the credibility of our opponents. Remember, everyone knows how to read non-verbal communication but few know how to write it.

CHARLIE GIBSON'S NON-VERBAL DISPLAY OF DISMISSIVENESS AND SUPERIORITY DIRECTED AT GOVERNOR SARAH PALIN

Visit http://tinyurl.com/gibsoninterview to watch.

Notice that comrade Gibson is literally looking down his nose at Governor Palin. Propping reading glasses on the end of one's nose is a classic non-verbal cue designed to convey intellect and superiority. Also, please take note of the facial expression Mr. Gibson makes immediately after he asks his first question. This micro-expression of sneering leaked out and tells you everything you need to know about how Mr. Gibson truly feels about Governor Palin. This proves his loyalty to our cause. Watch closely as the director calls for a "tighter shot" to focus upon the uncomfortable guest's face. The end result was that Governor Palin was put on the defensive.

Governor Palin fell prey to our sympathizer's intimidation and fell right into our hands by trying to become more personal, friendly and "cute." Her winks and classic feminine attempts at charm were everything we could have hoped for her to display to the world.

In response to her attempt to charm her interrogator, she received from Mr. Gibson a flat affect, a stare and a cocked head. We should all learn to copy comrade Gibson's use of this classic non-verbal strategy designed to intimidate someone who, had she not been stopped, could have exposed our movement and potentially garnered enough support to aggressively come after us. This clip illustrates how we can exploit our enemy's lack of preparation and failure to protect its assets. Our enemy took a politician who was a star in the minor leagues and moved her into the "majors" before she was ready. The guest may not have been ready to play in the majors but we were. Governor Palin never fully recovered from this interchange.

Study the following still shots from the Gibson interview. Look closely at Mr. Gibson's scowling, condescending and superior facial displays; it will serve you well in all your interactions with our enemy. Also, learn to emulate our interrogator's postural alignment that conveys dominance and superiority. Pay close attention to the effect it had on our enemy. Palin is obviously cowed by Mr. Gibson's non-verbal displays.

"STILLS" FROM THE GIBSON INTERVIEW OF
GOVERNOR SARAH PALIN

Example No. 2: The display of giddy superiority and dismissiveness by using a fellow sympathizer's comedy sketch designed to make fun of Governor Palin.

CNN'S WOLF BLITZER AND JOHN KING RIDICULING
GOVERNOR SARAH PALIN

Visit http://tinyurl.com/blitzerking to watch.

In this video clip our operatives use classic techniques designed to protect their "serious journalist" facade all the while communicating through their non-verbal communication that the target of their assault deserves to be made fun of and dismissed. Operative Blitzer hides behind a comedy sketch. "It's not me, its SNL who made fun of Governor Palin."

Learn to emulate what is happening here. This is concocted drama and it works. The editorial decision to borrow a clip from a comedy show known to ridicule Conservatives was a brilliant decision. By using this technique Blitzer could plausibly deny that what he was doing was making fun of Governor Palin.

Pay attention to the noticeable laughter in the background. Think of this technique as serving the same function as a "laugh track" on a situation comedy. Use this tactic whenever possible. Pay close attention to the next video clip of our operative Katie Couric who brilliantly uses the same condescending non-verbal missives on Governor Palin as used by Mr. Gibson.

KATIE COURIC

Visit http://tinyurl.com/couricinterview to watch.

The "head cock," flat affect and subtle sneer is an effective non-verbal strategy to undermine an opponent of our revolution. If Miss Couric is scowling, skeptical and superior then the unconscious assumption made by viewers is that whomever she is questioning MUST BE deserving of those dismissive displays. As before, the ill prepared Governor Palin responded exactly as desired by comrade Couric.

You can rest assured that our non-verbal displays of superiority, dismissiveness and skepticism will have their desired effect. In Governor Palin's case she tried to charm her way out the situation. Others will become angry while some victims may lose their train of thought, become defensive or engage in any number of negative behaviors that will ultimately help our cause by making our target look unprepared, defensive or just plain stupid.

Finally, we want you to study the non-verbal behavior of Vice President Joe Biden as displayed during the 2012 Vice Presidential Debates. Mr. Biden debated Congressman Paul Ryan.

Let me remind you that we are the masters of dramatic enactment and symbolic outrage. Our enemies are typically unprepared to deal with our drama-based psychological warfare. In fact, I will go so far as to say that our enemies have no idea what it is we are doing or the fact that we are engaging in this warfare at all.

For now, simply study how Vice President Biden dismisses Paul Ryan.

2012 VICE PRESIDENTIAL DEBATE BETWEEN JOE BIDEN AND PAUL RYAN

Visit http://tinyurl.com/ryanbiden to watch.

Ryan is an enemy of our revolution. He is known as a serious person, "wonkish," if you will, who needed to be diminished in the eyes of the electorate. Vice President Biden accomplished the task of diminishing Ryan by using the non-verbal sneer, condescending smile and dismissive non-verbal cues.

The examples we've presented demonstrate how we use non-verbal drama to subvert not only the electorate but our enemy as well. Consistent with our other victims, Ryan reacted to Biden by trying to muddle through the debate and by ignoring the obvious non-verbal psychological war being waged against him.

Next we present an effective non-verbal attack upon our mortal enemy, the TEA Party movement. Our operatives use our now classic set of dismissive non-verbal cues to undermine the TEA Party.

CNN REPORTERS SKEWER TEA PARTY MEMBERS

Visit http://tinyurl.com/tprally to watch.

You'll notice how the formal and professional introduction to the story ends abruptly and our operative's non-verbal assault begins with a joke and a dismissive laugh. Next, you'll see that comrade Roesgen searches out and targets the most vulnerable member of the TEA Party to attack using skeptical and dismissive non-verbal cues.

You may ask what was it about the TEA Party member that attracted Roesgen to him? Our opponents are often stupid and ignorant of the rules of psychological warfare. The TEA Party member targeted in the Roesgen clip combined an image of Hitler with President Obama. Whenever you see one of our opponents invoke an image of Hitler, Nazis or use the terms Fascist or Storm Trooper, you must pounce on the opportunity. Because our enemy is not psychologically sophisticated, this particular TEA Party member had no idea that by using the term "fascist" and invoking an image of Hitler, the electorate conflated the TEA Party WITH Hitler and Nazis.

Our agent Roesgen was brilliant at helping the viewer to conflate the underlying message of the TEA Party with actually being a Nazi. What occurs next in our drama-fest is that comrade Roesgen targeted a man with a child. This was a brilliant move on her part because her intent was to conflate the "use of a child" with a Nazi-like mob, thereby suggesting child abuse. It almost worked.

Now we can learn from comrade Roesgen's mistake. Can you guess what that mistake was? Roesgen became too verbal and confrontational as opposed to simply permitting the dramatic set-up to unfold like she and her in-studio allies had brilliantly designed. Operative Roesgen committed an error by revealing who she really is.

CHAPTER XXII
Questions and Answers

Q: Comrade, why must we hide our true identity? Are we not proud of who we are?

A: Just as we are not Marxists, but are Progressives, we can never reveal our true motives, intent or identity. Our enemy must be conquered mind-by-mind, piece-by-piece, never knowing anything except that we are people striving for tolerance, social justice and fairness. We will be able to Trojan-Horse every principle of Communism into the very fiber of our enemy until that point in time when we become the dominant political and social force. At that point we will declare who we are. By then, our enemy will be unable to do anything to stop us and prevent what we have in store for them.

Q: Comrade, sometimes we grow impatient. Why not simply make a big move that will kill our enemy once and for all?

A: Remember the story about the frog in the pot. The frog will never realize he is being boiled to death IF you put him in warm water and slowly, very slowly, increase the heat until he is boiled alive. Put the frog in hot water and he may jump out of the pot and get away.

Q: Comrade, sometimes I cannot believe how much we can get away with in plain sight. Is there any way I can learn to be more comfortable subverting my enemy knowing that what I am doing is there for all to see?

A: Back in mother USSR we used to play a game called "hide the thimble." The interesting thing about that game involved the requirement that the player hide the thimble in plain sight for all to see. You would be surprised at how well you can hide something in plain sight. If our enemy hits us with an otherwise unassailable truth we will call upon our comrades in the media-entertainment complex to perform jokes, skits and engage in satire of the truth. The threat will disappear. You will remain invisible because our enemy does not want to see you.

Q: Comrade, so this last point brings to mind my question about what techniques help us achieve control over our enemy?

A: Do not be reluctant to accuse your enemy of exactly what it is you are doing. If your enemy accuses you of demeaning him simply point to one of his party members who demeaned a protected class. If your enemy tries to make a logical argument by pointing to some harmful fact, turn it around on him and draw his attention to the fact that somewhere in his or his country's history, we see evidence of the same harmful act. Always stay calm, cool and collected. As stated earlier, embrace the accusation by performing a caricature of the allegation that is "over the top." Laugh it off by using the non-verbal strategies outlined in this operations manual. When your enemy becomes agitated you will appear to be even more reasonable. Remember, we will have created a citizenry that has no tolerance for stress or rancor. Be soothing and calming all the while your opponent raises his voice.

Q: Comrade, what is the biggest threat to our successful revolution?

A: Our movement is susceptible to a counter-revolution. Our movement's history has been plagued by counter-revolutionaries who have overcome our best efforts and, in the case of the USSR, actually dismantled virtually all of our work. In the past we helped to create these counter-revolutions by being too honest, strident and impatient. Our new strategy, and this goes back to the principle of being patient and making our moves in small, incremental steps, are designed to fly under the radar until our success becomes inevitable. Once we achieve final control, never fear, heads will roll and you will have the opportunity to exact revenge on the feckless Americans who so easily turned on their own country to help our cause. People who turned on their own country can't be trusted because if they did it to their own country they will do it to us.

Q: Comrade, Your last answer reminds me of what I have heard from our elder revolutionary leaders that the useful idiots will, in the last stages of our revolution, turn on us. What do we do with them?

A: America is full of nice liberals who believe our mantras of tolerance, fairness, justice and economic equality. Among those ranks of sympathizers are the sexual deviants and drug users who joined with us because we stand for sexual indulgence absent responsibility and Christian morality.

Once we take control we will need to eradicate these useful idiots. Once we become transparent and direct, the nice liberals who were so useful to our movement in its early and middle stages may revolt. Sexual deviants will have outlived their purpose once we take control. When that happens we will eradicate them unless, in the unlikely event, they re-educate themselves to see the wisdom of our methods and the stupidity of liberalism. As you may have already surmised, liberals are very easy to have your way with. These people turned on their own country to indulge their sexual deviance without control or guilt so how can you ever trust people like that? How can you trust people who supported the destruction of their own country?

Q: Comrade, what will become of those rural dwellers and Southern anti-Communists who will never join our movement?

A: History informs us that we have always had to deal with this problem. We shall do exactly as our former leaders have done, whether it was comrade Stalin or the great Mao, we will remove these citizens from the equation for the good of all. We shall be humane in our efforts, but we will be efficient, that I guarantee you.

Q: Comrade, is there anything that can be done to stop us?

A: Practically speaking the answer is no. But we could be stopped if Americans took to the streets and used our own methods against us. We could be stopped by the systematic purging of our operatives at all levels of government. The last time that was tried it was spear headed by one of our mortal enemies, Senator Joseph McCarthy. We have been so successful at stigmatizing his efforts in this regard that we have managed to introduce a new term into American lexicon: "McCarthyism". So if anyone tries to expose us to the point of purging us as anti-American or guilty of treason, we simply cry out our "safe" term "McCarthyism" and we will win. You see, our enemy has no stomach to do what would be necessary to defeat us.

Q: Comrade, do need we worry about a military coup?

A: Yes, we should always worry about any group with guns. This is why we have embarked upon our own purging of America's military leaders who could potentially pose a threat to our cause.

Q: Comrade, how do you purge military leaders?

A: By using the same techniques we have always used to purge anyone we chose not to outright kill, we assassinate their character. We use sex, drugs, gambling or any other vice you can think of. If a potentially dangerous military leader is not already engaged is an actionable vice, we introduce our femme fatale agents to subvert our threat. It is really quite easy.

We also are busy "watering down" of our enemy's military as we speak. We have been engaged in socially engineering away homogeneity in our enemy's military. This, alone, destroys cohesiveness. We have introduced sex into combat and we have taken young men full of testosterone and introduced gender identity issues for them to grapple with in addition to every other stress associated with being in the military. We have used one other tactic with great success, we prosecute military men who are effective soldiers and who do what great soldiers have always done, kill people and break things. We make our enemy's soldiers worry about two enemies, the identified enemy and their own government. These strategies will eventually destroy the mettle of our enemy's military forces. When all is said and done, we shall be the only ones left with weapons who are willing to use them.

Q: Comrade, our strategies and tactics seem to be at work everywhere, is this true?

A: Not everything that works in our favor was planned. We have always been vigilant and on the lookout for events and naturally occurring cultural changes that can be turned for our benefit. We have been accused, for example, of staging mass shootings of children to effectuate out gun control legislation. I can assure you we have never done that, but if we had I would never admit to it. But we were, on the other hand, ready to pounce on these events and use them to further our goals of stripping Americans of the guns. We have been lucky, but remember, luck is defined as when preparation meets opportunity.

Q: Why America?

A: America is unbelievably rich and prosperous. It is also powerful, that is why we want it. Keep in mind that these are the same characteristics that made it impossible to defeat America from the outside. That is why we chose to implode America, to turn it against itself. We are like the virus that has circumvented the host organism's immune system so that the target of the virus ultimately destroys itself from within.

CHAPTER XXIII
Survival Guide

1. Survival Guide: Stay clear of God fearing, humble people. Instead, give the microphone to Bible thumpers & let them preach.

2. Survival Guide: Encourage our opponents to nominate "pure" candidates that no one except them will ever vote for.

3. Survival Guide: We have magic phrases that make any threat disappear: "racist" "homophobe" "evangelical" "right winger" "intolerant" "hater."

4. Survival Guide: If our manual and network are exposed, simply cry "conspiracy theory nuts." The threat will disappear.

5. Survival Guide: Remember, a dumbed-down society is a supplicant society.

6. Survival Guide: Do not neglect biology. Encourage the use of mind numbing pharmaceuticals, legal and illegal. A doped country is a supplicant country.

7. Survival Guide: Remove all discipline from schools. When these students become adults they will embrace all things Progressive.

8. Survival Guide: Treat 10 year-olds like adults in all things, money, sex, politics and religion. As adults they will know nothing and be exclusively focused upon themselves.

9. Survival Guide: Begin awarding children with stars and trophies for simply showing up. They'll expect that when they become adults.

10. Survival Guide: Disconnect merit from awards. Make everything a popularity contest. Award those who "tow the line."

11. Survival Guide: Anoint your opponent's leaders. Make idiots their leaders by anointing them using our media friends.

12. Survival Guide: Socially engineer away the strength of the military. Use gender identity issues and sex to achieve that weakening.

13. Survival Guide: Purge leaders who may pose a threat to our movement. Study the Wizard of Oz and never let anyone pull back the curtain. If someone gets a peek then immediately marginalize him or her.

14. Survival Guide: Do "end runs" around strong opponents, e.g., promote reality TV that makes fun of Southerners & Christians.

15. Survival Guide: Don't worry about a "free press." We can simply ignore certain people. If that doesn't work, discredit them.

16. Survival Guide: Remember that everything we do is drama. It is a play for the masses, so always be a good actor.

17. Survival Guide: Never worry too much about people who speak the truth because the truth isn't as popular as lies and myth.

18. Survival Guide: Remember, while your opponents are glued to the TV you must be organizing and plotting your next move.

19. Survival Guide: Intimidate truth tellers using the psychology of "off limits speech." Gasp and act shocked if someone speaks truth.

20. Survival Guide: Promote multiculturalism by destroying the culture & religion of those who founded the country in your sights.

21. Survival Guide: Remember, your greatest allies are the useful idiots who believe they are geniuses because they are on TV.

22. Survival Guide: Be on the lookout for any national tragedy involving guns. Use that tragedy to confiscate guns.

23. Survival Guide: Partner w/Hollywood & the media. Conservatives will still pay for their cable and go to the movies regardless.

24. Survival Guide: Remember, people are stupid and if you can make them feel good you will win. Give them things & you will win.

25. Survival Guide: Never worry about conservative Twitter or Facebook mouths, they only talk, vent, gripe and complain while we work the system.

26. Survival Guide: Choose a front man who is charming, warm, witty and has a great voice. Someone who will tow the line no matter what.

27. Survival Guide: Dumb-down the country you want to take over. Fill the airwaves w/stupid people making big money.

28. Survival Guide: Use sex as your ally. Promote it, cheapen it, and turn it into a commodity. Make fun of people who are not libertines.

29. Survival Guide: Always put your focus on children. Use public schools to quietly indoctrinate kids and turn them against their parents.

30. Survival Guide: Help stupid conservative voices get the most air-time and make them media stars. Suppress intelligent conservative voices

31. Survival Guide: Fracture the society you want to take over into factions and groups; then pit them against one another.

32. Survival Guide: Foment class warfare by appealing to man's tendency to be jealous and envious. Promote entitlement.

33. Survival Guide: Shroud your Socialist agenda within a mantle of tolerance and fairness and justice for all.

34. Survival Guide: Keep pushing and pushing the collective agenda. Ignore/dismiss your opponents & never admit your true intent.

CHAPTER XXIV
The Elites

ANNA WINTOUR PROMOTES A FUNDRAISER FOR OBAMA

http://tinyurl.com/annawintourobama

Throughout this operations manual you have learned that man's nature can be one of our greatest allies in our efforts to subvert our enemy. Nowhere do we see man's nature as more helpful to our cause than when it comes to our natural allies, the elites.

Man likes to think of himself as better than his fellow man. He likes to think that he is superior, of a higher class, more intelligent, more beautiful, simply better. Societies throughout history have incorporated this tendency on the part of man to stratify into groups, with the "superior" group comprised of elites. Elite's walk, talk and possess affected mannerisms. Their affectations betray who they think they are in the grand scheme of life. And as remarkable as it may seem to you, these people are our natural allies.

Our revolution rests upon this proposition; the proletariat is oppressed by capitalists. We hold as self-evident that we know better than the common man and it is through our power that we will stand up for the "little man" and take from the rich man that which is rightfully his. The brilliance of our strategy is that our philosophy has already been adopted by the elites. They agree with us that the proletariat is made up of "lesser" humans who need to have their affairs micro-managed for their own good. There exists another motivation for elites to join our efforts. By helping our movement elites can continue to live like kings and queens while making it more difficult for those who would dare to try and gain membership in their club.

Our elites will come from fashion, the arts, Hollywood and the upper echelon of the investment community. The elites in this group live lives of privilege. They will identify with our revolution because theirs is a wealth born of image, inheritance, class and financial machinations, not scientific accomplishment, material creation (unless one considers creating a new hemline as a material creation) nor literary achievement.

Our elites are paid obscene amounts of money to act, sing, design, paint, primp and move money from here to there. We have news presenters among our ranks who earn $40 million dollars per year and investment fund heads who are worth tens of billions of dollars. We have no problem convincing them to pay more in taxes because what is a few extra million in tax revenue when you already have hundreds of millions, if not billions, of dollars?

Know this fact about elites: This class of humanity is comprised of cowards and social gadflies. They understand and fear that we are potentially threatening to them. We could, once we gain power, confiscate their wealth just as easily as we confiscate the small businessman's wealth. They know this and as an act of abject cowardice they become our 'friends," our supporters and financiers.

We are the masters of the semantic legerdemain, or slight of hand using words. The proletariat will identify with our elites because they, too, want to be like those who live like kings and queens, all the while parroting our slogans and our social engineering efforts designed to subvert our enemy. By supporting us the elites buy protection. Others support us because that assuages their guilt over having so much money for doing so little for the good of mankind.

Never forget that some of our elites are very, very wealthy businessmen. Only the wealthiest men and women are likely to become part of our revolution. This is because we represent a force even bigger than they. We are in a position to help them remain atop the business heap by engaging in what some have called crony-capitalism. Our supporters in certain businesses don't have to pay as much, if any, taxes or can count on the fact that we will reward them while punishing their competitors. In service to our revolution we are ready and willing to strike this deal.

Never forget that elites in the arts will gravitate to our movement because they, like us, know that the average American is too stupid to manage his own affairs. In return for their support we will reward them with admission to the greatest club of all time, membership in the ruling party's elite social clique. Never forget this, elites want to belong to the most prestigious club, group or clique, and our club is most elite of all.

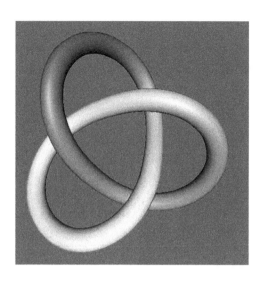

CHAPTER XXV
SUMMARY: Everything We Do Fits Together

Throughout this operations manual we have applied various psychological principles without actually describing what those principles are. We are now going to address the "glue" that holds our revolution together. As you continue reading always keep this in mind: Psychological warfare *is* war.

You may have noticed that image trumps substance in everything we do. We are the masters of drama and manipulating the symbols of social injustice. Let me give you an example that illustrates how drama wins over substance. Let's take our comrades in Hollywood to make this point. Never mind that many of our most vocal show business comrades live like kings and queens and have carbon footprints that would make "Big Foot" envious, they can still be, and in fact are, on the forefront of our Global Warming Movement because image trumps substance. These same men and women are supportive of our Occupy Wall Street movement. Almost to the person, Hollywood's elites are simpatico with the 99% and stand against the evil 1%, despite the fact that they belong to the top 1% of the evil 1%. Remember, it is not what you really are, it is what you say you are or look like that matters. And speaking of the dissonance between your symbolic expressions and what and who you really are, never fear the criticism of hypocrisy when it comes to the discordance between our dramatic enactments and reality. This is because when we act it out those images becomes more important than reality itself. You might ask: How is that possible?

We have taught teachers to teach that feelings and symbolic gestures are more important than reality. We have minimized the importance of reality by defining it as simply a word that refers to any one person's point of view or perception. Our psychologist comrades have helped us a great deal, as well, when it comes to convincing our enemy's citizens that feelings are more important than anything else is life. "How do you feel right now" has been the favorite mantra of psychologists and psychiatrists for over a half-century.

When you convince people that they are entitled to feel good at all times and that the most important thing in life is to feel good, you can easily stigmatize anything that disrupts man's quest for permanent pleasure. For example, if someone's feelings are "hurt" because he or she didn't win a race in grammar school, our comrade teachers have been taught to cultivate guilt in the winner and promote envy and jealousy in the losers. This has led to creating public school activities where there are no winners and losers. When there are no winners and losers everyone thinks they are entitled to be a winner, and in fact expects to be a winner. When

70

everyone feels entitled, we can step in and exploit the belief that our enemy has stolen your right to greatness. Entitlement minded citizens want redistribution of wealth as long as it flows to them, and that we will always promise. Our "favorite" capitalists become immune from our control IF they promise to finance and protect our efforts. We can use our "capitalist pets" as cover, pointing out to critics that "see, we have a good relationship with American business."

We benefit in another way when we train children to focus on feelings over everything else in their life, we create the framework for us to be able to censor speech we deem to be "hurtful." Truthful speech can kill our movement, so we can protect ourselves by defining truthful speech as hurtful or prejudiced speech. Or to say it another way, truthful speech hurts feelings and that makes it bad, and that means hurtful speech should be censored. We don't just limit ourselves to the children of our enemy we also modify macro-cultural norms.

America was, at one time, described as a melting pot. The idea was that immigrants from various cultures came to America and "melted" into becoming American. Our leaders identified the melting pot characteristic of America as posing a gigantic hurdle to our revolutionary goals. So what did we do? We turned the heat down on the melting pot.

We turned the heat down by first shaming Americans for having pride in their country. We took Conservative's children and mind-by-mind taught them that Columbus was an invader tyrant, that Pilgrims were oppressors, that America was bad from inception. Ask any American 7th grader what country was first to use germ warfare and they will say America, and point to our enemy's earlier settlers who used small-pox infested blankets to kill the native tribes of the new world. Did this really happen? No, our enemy America or any American agent never did this. Does it matter that America or its agents never engaged in this behavior? Not in the least. We must give special gratitude to comrade Howard Zinn who wrote "A People's History of the United States." Comrade Zinn's brilliant manifesto has turned two generations of Americans against their own country.

We have disallowed Americans to be American. We have shut down the Pledge of Allegiance. We have stopped prayer in schools. We began bi-lingual education after we dissolved America's borders and we have removed discipline from our public schools. That last point is an important one because along with the removal of virtually all discipline in schools we embarked upon treating children like they were adults. We encouraged 10 year-olds to take their place at the podium of life and expound on such issues as economics, sexual behavior, world affairs, family, marriage and politics. Children not mentally or fully physically developed were taught to believe their opinions and views were just as important as, for instance, a 50 year-old veteran of combat with a wife and 2 children. In short, we have created narcissistic personality disorder children who, because of their mental and physical immaturity, are drawn to our strategies and tactics. Conservatives have continued to finance both their children's illusions and our psychological warfare. It is beautiful, isn't it?

We have created a culture where teachers are afraid of children, parents are afraid of their own children, teachers are more like their students than they are other adults and anything that promotes a positive American identity is censored and can get you fired or ostracized. We have changed and are changing Americans to be like our forefathers in the revolution of old and our inspirational leaders from the 1960's.

One of our other grand macro-cultural successes has to do with our efforts at prolonging adulthood. In the 1950's our enemy's country was characterized by women who got married before they were 20 years-old and men of a similar age who became fathers and breadwinners. This social behavior was antithetical to our movement. So what did we do?

We enlisted the help of women who were masculine in their behavior and identity who felt ostracized by traditional America. Their motivation was personal but perfectly in sync with our grand desire to destroy the nuclear family of our enemy.

In an act of brilliance, these masculine women named themselves "feminists." Their goal was to make child rearing obsolete. They accomplished this by promoting birth control, abortion and an emphasis upon a career and a prolonged education. Our efforts were focused upon Anglo females who were targeted to have fewer and fewer babies. When they finally did have babies, they would be in their 30's and would be naturally limited by the number of children they could have.

Our successful efforts at convincing Anglo women to not reproduce meant that our enemy's culture would die out. Comrade Paul Erlich deserves the Hero of The Soviet Union medal for producing a manifesto in 1968 (Zero Population Growth) that made it "cool" to reject motherhood and fatherhood in favor of narcissism.

Some Conservatives and Liberals, alike, recognized the danger represented in this change in reproductive demographics. This provided the initial rationale toward increasing immigration from cultures that we would insure would not easily assimilate. The fact is Anglo America's birth rate is so low that it cannot sustain itself without the influx of legal and illegal immigrants. This is the product of our handiwork and has worked to our advantage, as many of these immigrants, many of whom are un-assimilating immigrants, have been strong supporters of our political strategies along with helping to destroy America's once vibrant identity.

Male Americans transitioned from young, responsible fathers into older metro-sexual males, many of whom live at home with their aging parents. Breadwinner fathers have been replaced with middle-aged men who have never been married, find the thought of fatherhood abhorrent and yet have proven to be some of our strongest supporters because we reinforce their sense of entitlement and perma-victim status. To be candid, we do not know what we are going to do with many of these demographic groups who have supported our movement once we take control of our enemy's country. In this sense, we are a victim of our own success. Our human behavior experts have concluded that even if many of our most strident supporters wanted to reform from their prolonged adolescence, their level of industry and usefulness will be too low to make them useable. Their arrogant attitudes will make them unsuitable once we take control. For now, that same arrogance makes them indispensable.

Our enemy has proven to be vulnerable to our psychological warfare strategies. We have come to realize that for any number of reasons Conservatives are not psychologically sophisticated. Many of them don't have the slightest idea about how psychological warfare is waged. We think that one of the reasons this is true has to do with something we mentioned in the very beginning of this operations manual. Traditional Americans have grown complacent; believing that the country they created would always exist as they designed it.

Many of those people who comprise Conservative's ranks do so because it fulfills their selfish and greed oriented lifestyle. These people are not patriotic Americans in the sense that they could not care less about America's documents or the principles found therein. Instead, what they care about is their own bottom line. These internationalist capitalists will not disagree with our revolutionary goals as long as we permit them to continue to accumulate wealth. Of course we can't do that because we need their capital to fund our movement, and therein is a significant point of friction.

These internationalist capitalists provide us with a wealth of ammunition in our psychological war because of their greed, avarice and megalomania. We have no problem lumping these people with true American patriots because typically they will vote for the same political class, despite the fact that they are as different as night and day. We should never make the mistake of confronting an American patriot when we can just as easily confront an internationalist megalomaniac to illustrate social injustice, unfairness, greed and avarice.

Along those same lines, we should never confront a true Christian person who lives their life in an unassuming, helpful and loving manner. Rather, we should use as foils tele-evangelists whose hypocrisy, megalomania, displays of opulent wealth and "creepy visual image" make them easy targets to undermine all of Christianity.

Be on the lookout for any scandal involving a Christian, especially an Anglo-Christian. Sexual abuse cases, homosexuality, thievery or adultery provide us a golden opportunity to undermine Christianity. Tele-evangelists who live like kings while offering salvation for seed money donations for special oils and cloths are perfect for our use. They are, almost always conservative in their politics. If we were stupid enough to believe in God we would most assuredly say: Thank you Jesus!

CHAPTER XXVI
Epilogue

Détournement is similar to satirical parody, but employs more direct reuse or faithful mimicry of the original works rather than constructing a new work, which merely alludes strongly to the original. It may be contrasted with recuperation, in which originally subversive works and ideas are themselves appropriated by mainstream media. One could view détournement as forming the opposite side of the coin to 'recuperation' (where radical ideas and images become safe and commodified), in that images produced by the spectacle get altered and subverted so that rather than supporting the status quo, their meaning becomes changed in order to put across a more radical or oppositional message.

My use of détournement against Marxists and their knowing or unknowing sympathizers is not only a literary technique you saw demonstrated in this book, it is a strong suggestion to you on how to confront and undo the insidious effects of the 50+ years of Communist demoralization and brainwashing of Americans.

Counter-revolutions typically begin with a small group of individuals who see through the strategies and tactics used by Marxists. These early adopter counter-revolutionaries see the writing on the wall if Marxists are allowed to continue their revolution without a counter-movement to stop them. So what constitutes a counter revolutionary? First, let's begin by identifying who is not a counter-revolutionary.

A counter-revolutionary is not merely a person who complains about what is happening to their country. Not "liking" what is happening to one's country is not the same as becoming expert on who, what, when, where, why and how America is being deconstructed, then engaging the battle. This is an increasingly important point given the saturation of social media in America.

Using social media to criticize and complain about the end results of Marxist strategies and tactics may even be counterproductive. This is because the act of complaining tends to delude the complainer into thinking that he or she has done something meaningful by complaining. Marxists are fully aware of those who don't like the end results of their efforts-the critics-if you will, but they don't care. And the primary reason they don't care is that complaining about things doesn't materially impact Marxist's push to subvert the country of their critics.

If one looks at the current political and social framework within which Marxists are effectuating their revolution, you will notice that lots of people complain. In response to these critics, the political operatives in the Progressive movement just keep on keeping on.

Upon the rare occasion that a particularly articulate critic of Progressivism manages to capture the public's attention, that person becomes a target for marginalization.

The tactics used to marginalize an articulate complainer are often invisible to the naked eye, but the end result is not. Cloaking one's subversion of threatening critics is one of the things that helps to make it successful.

Some may find it disturbing that Communists can, at times, actually benefit from their critics. This is because critics of Marxism and its sympathizers are typically not schooled in the ways of their enemy. Critics may be good, salt of the earth patriots, but they typically don't have the slightest bit of insight into how their criticisms can, and most certainly will, be used against them.

One of the narratives used against TEA Party members is that they are uneducated reactionaries. One of the tactics Communist sympathizers use to make that point is to single out TEA Party generated signs and placards that contain spelling errors. Here are a few examples actually used by Progressives in their marginalization efforts directed against the TEA Party:

These signs should never have passed muster with the counter-revolutionary expert in charge of signs. Of course, no such person exists, and that is one of the reasons Marxists were able to use these American patriot's well-intentioned efforts against them.

Peeling back the onion just one layer at a time exposes what is really going on here. Communists aren't really concerned about spelling mistakes. In fact, the use of misspelled TEA Party inspired messages has nothing, per se, to do with spelling errors at all.

The meta-communication intended by Communist sympathizers is that those who criticize them are stupid and uneducated. Pay close attention to the fact that Marxist sympathizers went out of their way to protect the things they hold most dear. By pointing out the tee shirt that reads "No to Socilis," Marxists exposed their sensitivity to criticisms made of Socialism. Marxists used a meta-communication to give the impression that people who say "no to Socialism" are so stupid they can't even spell "Socialism" correctly. What is truly instructive is that Marxist's reacted to the mere suggestion that America should say "no to Socialism." This means that Marxists are worried about attacks upon the precepts of Socialism and/or that they would be properly identified as just that-Socialists.

The poor fellow who misspelled the word "moron" was stupidly accusing his Communist enemies of being stupid. We say "stupidly" accusing his enemies because when you bring up intelligence you should probably make sure that your behavior connotes intelligence.

An even more ominous counter attack currently being waged against the TEA Party involves the psychological operation of re-defining the TEA Party as a militant militia that warrants military response preparedness. In January of 2013 the United States Department of Homeland Security funded a counter-insurrection training mission that pitted the

United States Army against an imaginary TEA Party militia group.

Retired Army Colonel Kevin Benson and history professor Jennifer Webber put together a hypothetical insurrection fantasy that cast the TEA Party as a guerrilla military force. In Benson's and Webber's deadly serious drama, entitled: **The Army Operating Concept 2016-2028**, a TEA Party guerrilla army takes over a South Carolina town, arrests the mayor and dismisses the police chief, county sheriff and disbands the city council. In this science fiction drama that would be ludicrous if not gravely serious, the TEA Party governor appoints himself mayor and after failed attempts to reason with this TEA guerrilla group, the United States Army is sent in to eradicate the TEA party guerrilla fighters and their sympathizers.

The TEA Party's main focus has always been limited government. No criminal or civil prosecution has ever been necessary at a TEA Party event, which have been attended by tens if not hundreds of thousands of non-littering Americans exercising their Constitutional right of free assembly. Whether you agree with the notion of limited government or not, wouldn't you conclude that if any group poses a threat to civil tranquility it would be the Occupy Wall Street Movement? That movement was confirmed to have within its ranks people who plotted to blow up bridges in Ohio, committed any number of assaults, rapes and included the utter destruction of public lands for weeks on end to the tune of hundreds of thousands if not millions of dollars' worth of damage. None other than the current President of the United States has expressed simpatico with the Occupy movement.

The approval of Benson and Webber's dangerous mischaracterization of The TEA Party illustrates quite vividly how threatening *talk* of limiting government truly is to Progressives. Higher taxes and an ever-expanding Federal government is its life's blood. The TEA Party never understood the bone chilling threat limited government posed to Progressives and their revolutionary goals. It should be abundantly clear that if the United States is willing to go to war with a peaceful group whose claim to fame is that it petitions for limited government and that it cleans up after itself once its rallies are completed, that the Marxists in our government, just like their fathers and their fathers before them, play to win and play for keeps. Given Benson and Webber's funding by forces in our government, one must wonder if there are other active measures currently being taken against TEA Party members, patriot groups or benefactors of Conservative politicians. The Federal government has at its disposal any number of agencies with police and investigative power that could make life difficult for their enemies.

Another hot-button issue for Communists is multiculturalism. They know they must dissolve America's culture before they can impose their collective control. This is why Marxists targeted the Village of Crestwood's "no excetions" (sic) sign. Marxists need to portray those who would defend America's cultural heritage as stupid. Again, from this spelling criticism we see proof positive that Marxists are very sensitive about anyone who would criticize multiculturalism. The lesson from the Crestwood sign is that exposing the dangers of multiculturalism should become a top priority for counter-revolutionaries.

Earlier in this book I cited comrades in the media-entertainment complex who targeted a TEA Party complainer who fell right into the hands of the reporter operative who pounced on him. You simply can't join images of Adolph Hitler, Nazi's and the President of the United States and hope that you won't do more harm than good to the counter-revolution.

Permit me to illustrate how sensitive you have to be when fighting the enemy. What if I had written the sentence above that began with the word "Earlier" and ended with the word "him," with this one modification:

> *Earlier in this book I cited comrades in the media who targeted a TEA Party complainer,* **a man who certainly had his heart in the right place**, *but who fell right into the hands of the reporter operative who pounced on him.*

The Marxist sympathizers who will read that last sentence will attempt to link me with images of Nazi's and Adolph Hitler by first showing the video clip of the TEA Party member holding up his Hitler and Obama sign, then the director will cut to the above passage in my book, then will ask with a cocked head, flat affect and dismissive tone: "So you think that it is OK Mr. Yevtushenkov to invoke images of Hitler when protesting the President of the United States?" They would be hoping that I would be offended at such a dismissive question and, like Governor Palin, be sensitive enough to try to undo their mischaracterization of me. The more I would deny the more vulnerable and off-kilter I would look. This is what the talking head sympathizers come to expect. It is their shtick. In their dreams they would broadcast a tight shot of me looking befuddled and unsure for a minute or so then they would immediately cut to an "expert" who is a Marxist sympathizer who will roundly criticize me in front of the nation for promoting hate.

How is it that counter-revolutionaries fall prey to these traps? Continuing with the above scenario, the producer of the hypothetical show would have contacted me to appear as a guest. He or she would have said nice things about my book and how this network or host wanted to interview me. This person would play to my ego and desire for attention. I can guarantee you, because I've been there and done that, the host will be beautifully lighted with professionally done makeup and I will be shot in "high key lighting" to wash me out. Once I sit down for the interview I will be sideswiped by manipulative questions and a barrage of host generated non-verbal cues designed to diminish me. Now because I know all of these things I don't fall prey to these tactics, but then again, I'm an expert at Communist skullduggery and I'm hoping that by studying this operations manual that you, too, will no longer be an unwitting victim.

So if complaining is bad, what then do we do? We fight fire with fire and we stop playing the role of unwitting victim. For instance, let's again reference the TEA Party members who were singled out to be foils for the Communist sympathizer from CNN who took them apart in front of the entire world.

Here are some rules: No TEA Party member can create a sign without it first passing muster with an expert who is a bona fide American counter-revolutionary educated in the ways of détournement. Next, TEA Party organizers should do exactly what Communist operatives do, ONLY allow trained spokespersons to interact with a potentially hostile questioner. Nowadays, Communists don't worry so much about tough questions because they have managed to infuse the mass media with sympathizers to the point where a Progressive can virtually count on softball questions from any reporter working for one of the broadcast networks or any cable outlet, save for FOX, at least for now.

When I advise fighting fire with fire I have two major counter-operations in mind. The first counter-operation involves the surgical application of humor and détournement. Let's take Governor Palin who was ambushed by two notable sympathizers in America's version of the USSR's Izvestia and Pravda, Charlie (Mr. Granny Glasses) Gibson and Katie (The Meg Ryan Smile) Couric.

"Don't be so touchy Charles and Katie, it is all in good fun. Can't you take a joke, come on."

The very moment Charlie Gibson propped his glasses on the end of his nose, cocked his head and looked down (literally) on Governor Palin with a flat, condescending non-verbal display, Governor Palin should have been prepared to say the following: "Charlie, before we begin, are you trying to intimidate me with your impression of an old-curmudgeon, wearing those granny glasses?" The governor should have then reached over, taken the glasses gently off his nose, put them on, then with her feminine charm said, "OK, now let's begin because if anyone if going to be the granny here, it's going to be me."

Governor Palin and the rest of the nation would have been witness to an empty suit who would have been stripped naked and put on the defensive. Governor Palin would have immediately handed the glasses back to Gibson, then said: "Now I understand you have some questions for me." The Governor from Alaska would have won over the hearts and minds of everyone watching. Governor Palin's display of détournement would have turned the tables on her interrogator and exposed the psychological warfare being waged against her. Should Governor Palin have been better prepared? Of course she should have been better prepared.

I have always believed, as previously mentioned, that Governor Palin was called up from the minor leagues before her maturation time. I would have preferred to see her develop her political skills, travel the world, meet with leaders across the globe and prepare herself for the inevitable attacks from a Progressive infested media once she walked upon the national political stage. In keeping with my analogy, however, even the most talented minor league star, and the governor was a star, would find it almost impossible to turn down an opportunity to play in the majors. That was her mistake. Those who brought her "up" too fast should bear the majority of the blame for putting her in this situation in the first place.

When Katie Couric asked Governor Palin what newspapers she regularly reads, she should have stopped the slow walking interview, turned toward Katie and said this: "Katie, what makes you think that a conservative woman from Alaska can read?" Let's see what snappy comeback the former high school cheerleader Couric would come up with. The Governor should then follow with this quip: "The only paper I religiously read, front to back, is The Atlanta Journal Constitution." What Governor Palin will get from that answer is an immediately disarmed Couric. This is because Couric's father worked for that paper when she was growing up. The governor should then say the following, as she tones down the humor and speaks: "I read everything from the New York Times to the Washington Times. I sample the foreign press and when I have some spare time I love to read cookbooks and the National Rifleman." That would have been that. Should a Vice Presidential candidate actually read all of those papers? Yes.

Everyone knows that Couric's Meg Ryan-like smile is a significant part of her career cache, that and the fact that the "suits" who study such things tend to hire news readers whose image suggests that she will be a good fit for the people living in the "fly over states." Miss Couric made it in a business that emphasizes image over substance and frankly, none of us should be all that impressed with a news reader who reportedly makes $40 million dollars a year who relies upon smarter people to construct questions for her to read off a teleprompter and who prompt her to appear to be more knowledgeable and intelligent than she really is by talking to her live in her earpiece. Is Couric telegenic? You bet. Is Couric easy to listen to? Yes. Does Couric have an agenda? Without a doubt.

We're not disrespectful of Miss Couric, but we are not going to treat her as though she or any other news reader (presenter) is a heavyweight in the grand scheme of things. The fact that Ms. Couric has gotten away with her anti-Conservative détournement over the years was only made possible by the stranglehold Progressives have on America's media-entertainment complex. She is a star in a profession that is predominantly image over substance, where newsreaders call themselves "anchors" (as if to connote substance and weight) and who typically make more money than ER physicians who truly are anchors in their community because they serve humanity and save lives.

The demure image Miss Couric presents to the world is not the whole truth, both in terms of how she really looks and behaves. Here are some photos of Miss Couric without her stage makeup, flattering lighting and demure behavior put on for the camera.

To understand Katie Couric and her use of intimidating non-verbal communication when talking to opponents of her ideology, I am going to show to you a video of Miss Couric talking to a man who shares her particular political ideology. On May 1, 2010 a potentially devastating car bomb was discovered in New York City's Times Square on a busy Saturday night after the bomb "fizzled" and failed to detonate. Times Square was teeming with tens of thousands of people enjoying their night out on the town.

Before the crime had been solved, a demure, made-up and helpful Katie Couric interviewed Mayor Michael Bloomberg. As you watch the following interview notice how Couric stands with her hands draped in a passive and receptive pose. Also take note of the fact that when the Mayor can't find the right word, the ever helpful and receptive Couric helps New York's Mayor choose his words. What an interesting word choice, Ms. Couric.

KATIE COURIC INTERVIEWS NEW YORK MAYOR MICHAEL BLOOMBERG

Visit http://tinyurl.com/mbloomberg to watch.

Take special note of the staged drama between Couric and Bloomberg. Remarkably, but not surprising, the two operatives spewed a hateful and divisive speculation that the would-be killer of thousands of people on a Saturday night in Times Square may have been a "homegrown terrorist," someone who may have been opposed to Obama Care.

As you can see and hear, it was Couric, the helpful and gracious version, not the dismissive shrew who skewered Governor Palin, who volunteered the word "homegrown." What we learned, of course, is that the would-be mass murderer was a Pakistani born Muslim terrorist, a Jihadi, who was intent upon killing Americans in the name of Islam. It was not a "homegrown" White man who disagreed with President Obama's Patient Protection and Affordable Care Act. Why did I say "White man?"

Bloomberg's office and the media-entertainment complex had widely publicized surveillance footage of a White man seen walking in the area of Times Square. Watch the following ABC News report that uses the descriptor "White man" repeatedly.

ABC NEWS REPORT ON TIMES SQUARE BOMBER

Visit http://tinyurl.com/squarebomber to watch.

88

Watch as the same media outlet loathe to use the descriptors Islam, Muslim or Arab, has no problem implicating an innocent White man who simply removed an outer sweater on a hot day and placed it in his satchel.

Note that the "anchors" read from a teleprompter where it had been written that the innocent man "stuffed" his outer shirt in a bag. Later in the report, despite the fact that Jihadi's took credit for the attempted terrorist attack, the point is made that the U.S. government doesn't believe Islamist's take-credit message. When you disassemble the hate filled prejudice and manipulation displayed here, with emphasis upon a compliant and helpful media-entertainment complex operative like Katie Couric and others, you can clearly see that America is awash in an orchestrated effort to manipulate cognitions, emotions and ultimately behaviors at the expense of the truth.

This report, paired with Bloomberg's and Couric's hateful speculative screed, and you have a Progressive psychodrama worthy of an Oscar. In the minds of the unwitting public, and I presume Miss Couric, this poor soul shown removing his outer sweater on a hot day *was the suspect*. However, every forensic expert with any experience knew that **everything** about the Times Square mass bombing attempt had Jihadi terrorist written all over it. So what is the truth?

Faisal Shahzad declared his motivation to commit mass murder in Times Square to Federal Judge Miriam Cederbaum. As you read Shahzad's words reflect upon Couric's interjection of the term "homegrown" and the insulting and manipulative nature of her use of that term along with the White man wrongly targeted by the media-entertainment complex:

New York Daily News:

> *"it's war," Shahzad, 30, said in a hateful screed to Manhattan Federal Judge Miriam Cedarbaum. "I'm going to plead*

guilty a hundred times over because until the hour the U.S. pulls its forces from Iraq and Afghanistan and stops the drone strikes...we will be attacking the U.S.," he said. "And I plead guilty to that."

Counter-revolutionaries are the people who pull back the curtain on the subversives within their midst and in so doing expose their brainwashing strategies and tactics for all fair-minded men and women to see. And speaking of pulling back the curtain, here is a video clip that serves as a metaphor for how a counter-revolution typically begins:

WIZARD OF OZ "CURTAIN" SCENE

Visit http://tinyurl.com/ozcurtain to watch.

In real life the wizards don't so quickly cave-in and admit to who they are and what they are up to. Marxists have put into place fail safe protections against discovery by the forces of good that would expose them for what they are. One way to process much of the content of this book is to think of it as an expose´ that reveals the Marxist firewalls used against counter-revolutionary's efforts to pull back the curtain. Most notably, Verboten!

Political correctness enforcement is the Marxist's front line weapon against a counter-revolutionary who would dare to pull back the curtain. Marxist operatives have been very successful at stigmatizing certain words and phrases. This stigmatization functions as a pre-emptive strike against any

90

threat that would dare to expose their movement or identify them as subversives. Two stigmatized terms that are important to study are "McCarthyism" and "Conspiracy." We've touched briefly on both but will now study how these terms are used in more detail.

Joseph McCarthy was a Senator from Wisconsin during the 1950's who spearheaded successful "uncover and roust" operations against Communist subversives within the United States. You can immediately see that the uncovering and rousting of Communist subversives would pose a potentially deadly threat to Marxist operatives and their designs on America. As was covered in detail in a book entitled: The Progressive Virus, Marxists always work in stealth mode to effectuate their revolution. They hide behind the mantle of social justice, fairness and equality all the while they are busy dismantling American principles and values and replacing them with Communist slogans, propaganda and social engineering strategies.

The stigmatized label "McCarthyism" is reserved for viable threats that may expose and roust Progressive subversives within our government and America's institutions. When Senator McCarthy made his efforts he confronted Communist threats that, when compared to today, were not nearly as serious both in number and extent, despite the powerful influences of the USSR at that time. Today, Socialists have infiltrated virtually every American institution. Avowed members of the Communist party have made their way into the highest offices of America, including the White House.

Take the time to read the following article that appeared in the English version of Russia's Pravda news. Please recall that during the golden years of the USSR, Pravda and Izvestia were the government's official lap-dog media outlets. Counter-revolutionaries in The Soviet Union were fond of saying this: "There is no Pravda (truth) in Izvestia and no

Izvestia (news) in Pravda." After the second great Russian revolution, Pravda has now taken on the mantle of America's once objective media, that is, before it became the new lap-dog media outlet of the current regime in America.

OBAMA'S SOVIET MISTAKE

`19.11.2012 15:23`

`By Xavier Lerma`

Putin in 2009 outlined his strategy for economic success. Alas, poor Obama did the opposite but nevertheless was re-elected. Bye, bye Miss American Pie. The Communists have won in America with Obama but failed miserably in Russia with Zyuganov who only received 17% of the vote. Vladimir Putin was re-elected as President keeping the NWO order

out of Russia while America continues to repeat the Soviet mistake.

After Obama was elected in his first term as president the then Prime Minister of Russia, Vladimir Putin gave a speech at the World Economic Forum in Davos, Switzerland in January of 2009. Ignored by the West as usual, Putin gave insightful and helpful advice to help the world economy and saying the world should avoid the Soviet mistake.

Recently, Obama has been re-elected for a 2nd term by an illiterate society and he is ready to continue his lies of less taxes while he raises them. He gives speeches of peace and love in the world while he promotes wars as he did in Egypt,

Libya and Syria. He plans his next war is with Iran as he fires or demotes his generals who get in the way.

Putin said regarding the military,

"...instead of solving the problem, militarization pushes it to a deeper level. It draws away from the economy immense financial and material resources, which could have been used much more efficiently elsewhere."

Well, any normal individual understands that as true but liberalism is a psychosis. O'bomber even keeps the war going along the Mexican border with projects like "fast and furious" and there is still no sign of ending it. He is a Communist without question promoting the Communist Manifesto without calling it so. How shrewd he is in America. His cult of personality mesmerizes those who cannot go beyond their ignorance. They will continue to follow him like those fools who still praise Lenin and Stalin in Russia. Obama's fools and Stalin's fools share the same drink of illusion.

Reading Putin's speech without knowing the author, one would think it was written by Reagan or another conservative in America. The speech promotes smaller government and less taxes. It comes as no surprise to those who know Putin as a conservative. Vladimir Putin went on to say:

"...we are reducing taxes on production, investing money in the economy. We are optimizing state expenses.

The second possible mistake would be excessive interference into the economic life of the country and the absolute faith into the all-mightiness of the state.

There are no grounds to suggest that by putting the responsibility over to the state, one can achieve better results.

Unreasonable expansion of the budget deficit, accumulation of the national debt - are as destructive as an adventurous stock market game.

During the time of the Soviet Union the role of the state in economy was made absolute, which eventually lead to the total non-competitiveness of the economy. That lesson cost us very dearly. I am sure no one would want history to repeat itself."

President Vladimir Putin could never have imagined anyone so ignorant or so willing to destroy their people like Obama much less seeing millions vote for someone like Obama. They read history in America don't they? Alas, the schools in the U.S. were conquered by the Communists long ago and history was revised thus paving the way for their Communist presidents. Obama has bailed out those businesses that voted for him and increased the debt to over 16 trillion with an ever-increasing unemployment rate especially among blacks and other minorities. All the while promoting his agenda.

"We must seek support in the moral values that have ensured the progress of our civilization. Honesty and hard work, responsibility and faith in our strength are bound to bring us success."- Vladimir Putin

The red, white and blue still flies happily but only in Russia. Russia still has St George defeating the Dragon with the symbol of the cross on its' flag. The ACLU and other atheist groups in America would never allow the US flag with such religious symbols. Lawsuits a plenty against religious freedom and expression in the land of the free. Christianity in the U.S. is under attack as it was during the early period of the Soviet Union when religious symbols were against the law.

Let's give American voters the benefit of the doubt and say it was all voter fraud and not ignorance or stupidity in electing a man who does not even know what to do and refuses help from Russia when there was an oil spill in the Gulf of Mexico. Instead we'll say it's true that the Communists usage of electronic voting was just a plan to manipulate the vote. Soros and his ownership of the company that counts the US votes in Spain helped put their puppet in power in the White House. According to the Huffington Post, residents in all 50 states have filed petitions to secede from the Unites States. We'll say that these Americans are hostages to the Communists in power. How long will their government reign tyranny upon them?

Russia lost its' civil war with the Reds and millions suffered torture and death for almost 75 years under the tyranny of the United Soviet Socialist Republic. Russians survived with a new and stronger faith in God and ever growing Christian Church. The question is how long will the once "Land of the Free" remain the United Socialist States of America? Their suffering has only begun. Bye bye Miss American Pie! You know the song you hippies. Sing it! Don't you remember? The 1971 hit song by American song writer Don McLean:

"And, as I watched him on the stage my hands were clenched in fists of rage.

No angel born in Hell could break that Satan's spell

And, as the flames climbed high into the night to light the sacrificial rite, I saw...

Satan laughing with delight the day the music died

He was singing, bye bye Miss American Pie

Drove my Chevy to the levee, but the levee was dry

Them good ol' boys were drinking whiskey and rye, singing...

This'll be the day that I die

This'll be the day that I die

So, the question remains:

How long will America suffer and to what depths?

Xavier Lerma

Contact Xavier Lerma at
xlermanov@swissmail.org

His popular articles can be seen at
http://xlerma.wordpress.com/

Hyperlink to Pravda is mandatory if you republish this
article.

If any news organization knows what Communist infiltration looks like it is Pravda.

Consider why American-Communist subversives did not accuse Pravda of engaging in "McCarthyism?" PRAVDA IS RUSSIAN and its credibility when it comes to identifying Communists is beyond reproach, even for America's subversives who usually couldn't care less about attaching an unwarranted stigmatized label. You saw how I applied the strategy of using unassailable sources when I began this book with a video clip of Yuri Bezmenov, the ex KGB agent who defected to America in the 1980's.

Another reason Marxist operatives didn't cry "McCarthyism" by criticizing Pravda is that they trust that the American voter will seek out news about Beyonce and Jay-Z but not an editorial from a Russian newspaper that declares that America is infested with Communists, including the White House. I'm using CNN's tactic used against Governor Palin, "it's Pravda, not me, that has asserted that the current inhabitants of the White House are Communists." I actually do believe that Pravda is in a better position to assess who is and who is not a Communist or Communist sympathizer, especially given their unequaled first-hand experience with Communists, Socialists and Progressives.

The counter-revolutionary strategy illustrated here is to align yourself with Pravda and its journalists. You should have, at the ready, an iPad loaded with the original story that provides protective cover when America's Communist sympathizers and operatives start throwing around stigmatized labels at America's counter-revolutionaries.

Permit me to repeat, I specifically recommend carrying with you at all times an iPad loaded with your unassailable proof in the form of original stories, photos, video clips and other supportive data that will serve as the ammunition for your counter-revolutionary détournement. If you are going to subject yourself to an interview with a media-entertainment complex operative, have that person's on-air history at the ready to play on your iPad at the drop of a hat.

One of the things counter-revolutionaries should immediately begin compiling is a bulletproof bank of unassailable data, including video, original sourced stories, statistics from official U.S. and/or Russian agencies. With reference to that last point, we should welcome whistle-blowers who are currently or have worked within America's Communist/Progressive network.

You've heard of the old saw "familiarity breeds contempt." That wisdom is never truer than when working around and with Communists and their sympathizers. Whether it is because Socialists ascribe to the end justifies the mean credo of social interaction, are atheists, are hedonists, passive-aggressive or simply because they are dissatisfied and obnoxious people, you can count on the fact that Communists don't make it easy to work for or with them.

Our welcome mat should always be out and we should actively solicit Progressive insiders to "see the light" and expose their comrades, within the confines of the law, for who they really are and what they are up to. We are especially interested in Communist's documents and internal memoranda. Here is one final thought regarding Communist whistle blowers. Many Conservatives were once card-carrying Liberals who saw the light by virtue of the fact that they worked around the obnoxious people who comprise Progressives and their sympathizers.

The second most popular stigmatized set of labels used by Communists and their sympathizers are the terms "conspiracy," "conspiracy theory," "conspiracy nut." It is remarkable but very telling that a term that is so innocuous on its face would garner so much attention from Communist subversives. A conspiracy is simply this: *Two or more people working in unison and in a clandestine manner to achieve a common goal that is either illegal or subversive of another group, organization or ideology.* The noun Conspirator(s) refers to a person or persons involved with or engaged in a conspiracy. The term connotes a clandestine coordinated effort as opposed to a forthright effort among two or more people to achieve a common goal. Human beings are social animals and it is the rule, not the exception, that people desirous of achieving important goals coordinate their efforts to achieve those goals.

In the book The Progressive Virus the author analyzed the personality characteristics of Progressives using clinical data and insight. Communists are more likely to work in groups because the personality types who are drawn to Communism are, by constitution, attracted to working in groups, packs and mobs. The term itself "Communism" connotes the collective, the commune.

The Communist revolution currently taking place in America, in addition to each and every other Communist revolution of the past 100 years, was a conspiracy in every sense and meaning of the term. The conspirators in each and every one of these Communist revolutions made great efforts at hiding the fact of their conspiracy. The reasons for this are twofold.

In the first instance, if you reveal to the existent power structure that you are engaged in a conspiracy to overthrow that existent power structure, you may find yourself behind bars or worse. The second reason for creating a stealth conspiracy is that if the existent powers and the citizens of the targeted nation really understood that a group of conspirators were working to install a Communist state, with all of its control, regulation and confiscation and redistribution of wealth, there may very well be a counter-revolution. Communists have been successful at undermining the credibility of those who would expose the conspiracy among Communists in our government, institutions and media-entertainment conglomeration.

Let's take a look at a Progressive sympathizer's attack on a United States Senator that took place on February 24, 2013. This U.S. Senator became the target of Marxist inspired sympathizers because he had dared to challenge the appointment of Senator Chuck Hagel as Secretary of Defense. We'll dissect the tactics used against this Senator and expose just how devious the media-entertainment complex can be.

Here is the story from MSNBC:

TED CRUZ STICKS WITH MCCARTHYISM CLAIMS

Amanda Sakuma, @iamsakuma
12:13 PM on 02/24/2013

"Texas Republican Ted Cruz is not denying his red scare tactics–in fact, he's doubling down on them. After the freshman senator made a brash first impression during defense secretary nominee Chuck Hagel's confirmation hearing, recently unveiled comments from Cruz's past reveal that the innuendo-laced line of grilling directed at Hagel was not the first time Cruz was reminiscent of Sen. Joseph McCarthy's anti-communist witch hunt."

Let's begin our analysis by focusing upon the photo used by MSNBC. This photograph of Senator Cruz is about as unflattering as unflattering can be. MSNBC chose a photograph that still-framed an articulate Senator Cruz right at the moment his mouth was agape, his head was off-kilter and at that precise moment Senator Cruz' facial affect looked "stupid." To see just how easy it is to take ANY video of virtually ANY person and select from that video a still frame that makes the subject of the video look stupid, try it by selecting a still frame from a video of one

Republican candidate for U.S. Senate Ted Cruz answers a question from a television reporter Tuesday, Nov. 6, 2012, in Houston. (AP Photo/David J. Phillip)

of your friends or yourself that makes YOU or your friend look bad.

Now let's focus upon the stigmatized terms used in just the first paragraph of the story. The story is chock full of loaded terms designed to stigmatize Senator Cruz. The terms were taken from MSNBC's bank vault of stigmatized descriptors designed to destroy the credibility of a threat. This tactic comes right out of the Marxist playbook. I will highlight MSNBC's attempts at psychological warfare by underlining their stigmatized labels used within the first paragraph of their hit piece:

*"Texas Republican Ted Cruz is not denying his **red scare tactics**-in fact, he's **doubling down** on them. After the freshman senator made a **brash** first impression during defense secretary nominee Chuck Hagel's confirmation hearing, <u>recently unveiled</u> comments from Cruz's past reveal that the **innuendo-laced** line of grilling directed at Hagel was not the first time Cruz was reminiscent of Sen. **<u>Joseph McCarthy's anti-communist witch hunt</u>**."*

MSNBC exposed their true agenda by their use of terms designed to slur an opponent of their Progressive brethren. "Anti-Communist" paired with "Witch Hunt." "Red Scare Tactics." Isn't it fascinating that any anti-Communist comment is virtually always paired with the stigmatized label "Witch Hunt?" Just consider the issue from an academic perspective.

When a politician criticizes a political ideology like Communism, whose history would, at the very least, make it vulnerable to criticism, is that criticism ALWAYS a Witch Hunt? No, of course not. So why are the two terms virtually always paired by America's media-entertainment complex? Answer: Because Communists and their sympathizers are INTOLERANT of anyone who would dare to criticize and/or expose them for who they really are. You are NOT allowed, and if you do dare to criticize or threaten to expose them, you are systematically destroyed using every psychological warfare device and vicious character assassination tactic illustrated in this book.

All stigmatized labels attached to the enemies of Progressivism are designed to unconsciously elicit an affective negative valence. Bad people use scare tactics. None of us like to be scared in that way. So what MSNBC is really doing is conflating the fact of the public being justifiably scared by the issues Senator Cruz is raising with a premeditated attempt on the part of Senator Cruz to scare his audience in service to an ulterior motive.

It is MSNBC that has an ulterior motive to scare its readers and viewers, not Senator Cruz. In that respect, Socialists almost always use what clinical psychologists term "projection." Communists love to "project" upon their detractors the behaviors, traits and tactics that they possess or use. MSNBC projected upon Senator Cruz its own motive to skew perceptions through the use of scare tactics.

You will notice MSNBC's invocation of Joseph McCarthy's name as the intended tour de force smear on Senator Cruz. So permit me to dare ask the question, was Senator McCarthy correct in his central thesis that mid-century American Communists had their sights on overthrowing America and had, in fact, infiltrated many of America's institutions during Senator McCarthy's tenure in office? The answer is yes. Senator McCarthy was accurate when it came to his central thesis.

What follows is an interview with author M. Stanton Evans that took place in the summer of 2010. Evans wrote a book about Joseph McCarthy entitled: BLACKLISTED BY HISTORY: The Untold Story of Joe McCarthy. Evans uncovered unassailable data from official Russian and American intelligence agencies that demonstrate, beyond a shadow of a doubt, that Senator McCarthy was accurate in his central thesis. Yes, Evans was interviewed by Glenn Beck; and no dear Progressive, by including Beck's interview with Evans I'm not necessarily underwriting everything Beck says or does so don't yoke us together to impugn my integrity.

Not until after the fall of the USSR did we learn, definitively, what the Communists were up to in America during the cold war. When Senator McCarthy made his investigations he didn't have unbridled access to internal memoranda from Soviet intelligence agencies or from the F.B.I., he relied upon bits and pieces of data sets from inside sources.

AUTHOR M. STANTON EVANS INTERVIEW

Visit http://tinyurl.com/mstanton to

watch.

Senator McCarthy didn't have access to the inside information possessed by Yuri Bezmenov and a host of other former Soviet spies and operatives who constitute unassailable sources of data.

It turns out, according to unearthed Soviet and F.B.I. documents, that America's most important institutions had been targeted by Communists for takeover. During Senator

McCarthy's tenure, according to these official records, Communists had infiltrated government, the mass media-entertainment complex and were making inroads into America's public schools. And speaking of America's public school children, consider this.

Progressives have come to believe that public school children belong to them, not their parents. Many American children have been unwittingly abandoned by their parents who have turned over their children to Progressive indoctrinators (teachers) who are busy molding, shaping and brainwashing young minds to become secular humanist, anti-American martinets. When Progressives find a political leader with whom they can agree, they set about to brainwash immature minds to praise and engage in idolatry of that politician. Study the following video. It was taken within an American public school, paid for by your taxpayer dollars. What you see here is by no means rare.

PUBLIC SCHOOL CHILDREN BEING INDOCTRINATED

Visit http://tinyurl.com/pschildren to watch.

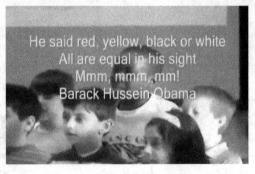

He said red, yellow, black or white
All are equal in his sight
Mmm, mmm, mm!
Barack Hussein Obama

Our comments and implied criticisms would equally apply to a Conservative politician or for that matter ANY politician. What you see demonstrated here should concern anyone, left, right, center.

These same children in this same school are forbidden to recite the Pledge of Allegiance or engage in a moment of prayer. They are forbidden to learn about American exceptionalism, say "Merry Christmas" celebrate Easter but they are trained in the practices of Kwanza, how Pilgrims exploited Native Americans and that the only differences between boys and girls are rooted in environmental examples of social injustice.

In 1963 Communist Party USA published a number of its long-term plans for America, including turning America's public schools into indoctrination camps, the removal of prayer in public schools, infiltration of the media/entertainment complex and the neutering of America's military using sophisticated psychological warfare strategies and tactics. What follows is a listing of 31 of Communist Party USA's goals for the takeover of America. The video was produced by *Constitutional Patriot.*

COMMUNIST PARTY GOALS CIRCA 1963

Visit http://tinyurl.com/communismgoals to watch.

Counter-revolutionaries should treat Marxists, Communists and their sympathizers as if they had been infected with a highly infectious, life-threatening disease. The ideology of the collective has always resulted in tyranny and abuses of personal liberty and freedom. Collectivist ideologies have been used as a justification to exterminate tens of millions of people who didn't "fit" the Communist/Socialist/Progressive/Marxist template. To understand Marxists one must become familiar with their motives.

Forensic experts spend a great deal of time deciphering motive. This is because once you have identified motive, you can then, and only then, make sense of world around you. Criminals can often hide or cover their physical tracks, but those same criminals have a much harder time shrouding their motive. Just like any subversive criminal, the goal is to avoid detection.

How many heinous crimes have been committed by people who broke into well- guarded buildings using a non-threatening disguise? How many prisoners have escaped from jail because they dressed like someone other than a prisoner and walked right out the front door? How may murders have occurred because an unwitting victim opened the door to someone dressed like a delivery person?

Communist subversives use disguises, as well. They dress themselves to look like middle-America. They rename themselves using words with inherent positive meaning, e.g., "Progressives," "Anchors," "Teachers," "Clergymen." They reframe their subversion into catch phrases that connote advancement, e.g., "moving forward" or "lean forward." They have faces that are chosen to look like "Middle America." They take jobs that used to be associated with patriotic America, e.g., public school teachers or reporters who once defined their job as keeping a wary eye on power. Communists stopped throwing bombs and began writing textbooks for public school teachers. And no one, it seems, caught onto this rather obvious, but devious, strategy.

Subversives also try to hide their motives. Their stated motives are classically unassailable and include noble pursuits like justice, fairness, equality and tolerance. In that regard they remind me of the genre of homicide mysteries involving nurses who took loving care of their elderly patients, except when they were busy killing those same patients with poison. But like all criminals, subversives can't keep their motives hidden forever, and sooner or later they will reveal their true identity. Counter-revolutionaries can help the process of revelation.

Understanding deep-seated motives provides insight into the Communist sympathizers among us. Think back to our chapters on "Elites" and "Non-verbal behavior." Recall that the media-entertainment complex was ruthless and unabated in its attacks on Governor Palin. I exposed the elites in that cabal of subversives and their use of non-verbal psychological operations designed to undermine their enemies. You'll notice that the enmity directed at Governor Palin was particularly vitriolic, beyond the pale. This is why.

The media-entertainment complex is comprised of self-anointed elites. One only need look at the behavior of the poster-child for the elite's superiority affectation, Anna Wintour, to understand that the reason Governor Palin was so viciously and mercilessly attacked is that she was not a card carrying elite. She came from a working class background and, unlike many of the current crop of elites, never rejected her roots. Here is a woman who allowed herself to be filmed making homemade chili for her family in a modest kitchen. "Why, that is the behavior of a commoner." Sarah Palin's kitchen looks nothing like the multi-million dollar kitchens of the elite, but then again, Governor Palin actually uses her kitchen to prepare meals.

Here is a woman who gave birth to a special needs child and made no bones about the fact that she intended to be a mom to that child. Governor Palin's most unforgivable sin, besides posing a threat to Progressives, is that not only is she not an elite, even worse, she does not lust to become a member of their clique. And when you are not one of them, and you don't want to be like them; you are not good enough to make it on the national scene, period. Governor Palin was the living embodiment of everything feminists have extolled over the years. She was a "super woman" who managed to combine motherhood, a career and political service all the while being an attractive person who had not lost her femininity. Described this way, you can now see why the self-anointed elites hated her with a passion. Ask any man with whom he would prefer to have dinner, Sarah Palin or Anna Wintour. I suggest the safe bet would be to place your money on Sarah Palin. I purposely left out women in my hypothetical question because I am of the opinion that elite women are so consumed with jealousy over the governor's sex appeal that there would be no point in asking the modified question.

One goal of counter-revolutionaries must be to deny Progressive subversives the accolades they crave and must chastise those who give them respect they do not deserve. A counter-revolutionary must allow others to see Socialist sympathizers for who they really are, not who they say they are. We must be familiar with their acts of hypocrisy, who pays them and we need to have at the ready a compendium of all their comments made on and off the record. Those data should be carried with the counter-revolutionary whenever he anticipates speaking in public.

No, this is not a witch-hunt; it is a hunt for those who would impose tyranny on Americans and the rest of the free world. Counter-revolutionaries are fighting tyrannical forces, including the useful idiots who simply find it fashionable to identify with all things "Progressive." Collectivists have proven themselves to be, time and time again, intolerant human beings who destroy or at the very least undermine every single culture or country they come in contact with, and now they are trying to do it to America. *It is immoral and intolerable to tolerate those whose culture, politics, ideology and religion inevitably leads to intolerance and tyranny.*

One of the first goals of a counter-revolution is this goal: There shall be no peace for subversives who have enjoyed, up till now, protected and insulated lives, away from the citizens they intend to subvert to the power of their Progressive comrades. Counter-revolutionaries must become permanent fixtures in their mind. Counter-revolutionaries shall make them personally familiar with the tactics they so arrogantly use on patriotic Americans each and every day. If any of them retain a semblance of a conscience they must be made to come face to face with the disaster that awaits them if they transform America into their collectivist utopia.

Counter-revolutionaries must always obey the law, lest you fall prey to a counter-counter operation designed to discredit counter-revolutionaries. Pay all your taxes, don't hang out with prostitutes, don't be a drunk and, above all else, don't present yourself to be without flaws, holier than thou. "Preachy" isn't nearly as effective as charming persuasion. All human beings are works in progress. Many of us are flawed but we are trying. Never write anyone off completely. There exists salvation for anyone. Never forget that many of the useful idiots we must deal with have been brainwashed since they were in grade school, so have patience and try to help them overcome their brainwashing.

The personality types who are attracted to Marxism love the strategies and tactics described in this operations manual. Counter-revolutionaries, on the other hand, are not naturally predisposed to engage in psychological warfare. Well-adjusted and happy people generally want to live and let live. Counter-revolutionaries must overcome their natural tendency to live and let live. Their adversaries are meddlers, controllers, manipulators, prevaricators and above all else, they subscribe to a ruthless end justifies the means credo.

I encourage the student of this book to read The Progressive Virus. That book psychoanalyzed those attracted to Marxism and provided a detailed look into their personal and group psychology. Suffice to say, our adversaries are nothing like us. Therefore, you can't use your own perceptions, cognitions and emotional makeup as points of reference from which you can fully understand Communist, Marxist, Socialist or Progressive subversives. Just as in forensic psychology, to understand the crime and the criminal you have to become expert on how the criminal perceives, thinks about and emotionally reacts to the world around him.

Since personal responsibility is a lynch-pin value held dear by Conservatives, it behooves Conservatives to apply that noble principle in a way that will help their cause, and that would be to apply personal responsibility to themselves, their politicians and their benefactors.

In the détournement section of this book our Marxist trainer made it crystal clear that the enemy had within its ranks any number of unwitting Marxist allies who identified themselves as Conservatives or Republicans. Our trainer made it clear that given the choice between using as a foil a salt of the earth Conservative family man or an internationalist capitalist, tele-evangelist, Bible thumper, greed merchant or reactionary "gun nut" or jingoistic Republican, the Marxist student should steer clear of the salt of the earth family man. The list of suitable foils for Marxists is, interestingly enough, comprised of Republicans and/or people who label themselves Conservatives.

What I am conveying here is that Progressivism didn't just crop up as an abomination in a utopian world run by Conservatives and Republicans. Just as the arrogant abuses and wanton greed of the Czars of Russia set the stage for the

Bolshevik Marxists to initiate their Communist revolution, America's Progressives used some Conservative's greed, avarice and insensitivity to other's to motivate their revolution. Republicans, in particular, have been either unable or unwilling to take a critical look at their own behavior that set the stage for the current Progressive revolution taking place in America.

I recognize that labels are fraught with any number of built in limitations and can be used for nefarious purposes. As we have learned from our Marxist trainer, the use of stigmatized labels can be very effective when it comes to stifling truth telling. When used as shorthand identifiers, labels can be misused even though the intent of the user is not malicious. So it is with political labels. To illustrate this last point, let's examine the label "Liberal."

The Liberals of yesteryear would be considered Conservatives by 2013 standards. Jack Kennedy, Henry "Scoop" Jackson, Sam Nunn and featured speaker at the 2012 Republican Convention, Clint Eastwood, just to name a few, meet virtually all the criteria to be labeled Conservatives. However, these men are and were, in the traditional sense, Liberals.

Traditional Liberals, like the men identified above, possessed a political ideology that was 100% American. President Kennedy's beseech to "Ask not what your country can do for you but what you can do for your country" is pure traditional Americana. That plea is the diametric opposite of the Progressive's welfare state mantra that encourages government dependence and defines citizens as entitled to rely upon the government for not only their success but their daily sustenance. So what empowered Progressives? Here is just a sample of the kinds of things that empowered Progressives and fueled their movement.

Before Liberal sponsored child-labor laws were enacted the 10 year-old sons of the working poor were allowed, dare I say encouraged, to put in 18 hour days at the factory rather than attend school. While the rich kids were busy being tutored, chauffeured to their prep schools, the poor kids were helping to make some capitalists rich.

Before the Teamsters Union came along truckers were forced to drive until they dropped. Consider this, trucking companies sometimes failed to provide drivers with trucks that had working heaters, yet forced their drivers (that is, if they wanted to eat) to haul their loads in the dead of winter. If the truck broke down, as it sometimes would, the driver would freeze to death. Back in those days there were no cell phones or roadside emergency phones so you were literally on your own.

Capitalists and their Conservative political leaders of yesteryear were thoughtful enough to build "poor-houses" where the disabled truck driver and other workers too old or just plain worn out could live out the rest of their lives eating gruel and sleeping on surplus Army cots.

The point is worth repeating: Marxism didn't just crop up as an abomination in a utopian world run by Conservatives and Republicans. America's Progressives used some Conservative's greed, avarice and insensitivity to empower their revolution. And we should never forget that psychological manipulation is not the exclusive purview of Marxists. When such abuses are recognized for what they really are, that awareness provides an effective springboard from which one can launch a revolution.

Progressives are not the only one's who use staged political drama to modify voter's perception of reality. Who can or should forget "Mission Accomplished," a million-dollar plus political-drama staged off the coast of San Diego where President George W. Bush, dressed like Tom Cruise in the movie "Top Gun," sat in the back of an F-15 while a Navy pilot landed the fighter jet on the aircraft carrier Carl Vinson. Republican donors AND the American taxpayer paid for this staged drama. To this day any number of Conservatives believe, just as Karl Rove intended, that George W. Bush actually piloted that plane to a safe landing on the aircraft carrier Vinson.

Thousands of Americans either died or were seriously injured after the filming of Rove's staged political drama entitled: *Mission Accomplished.* The most recent scientific poll of Iraqi's taken in 2013 found that the vast majority despise America. Iraq's next-door neighbor, Iran, has grown exponentially in power since "43" made his fateful decision to invade Iraq.

Now to be perfectly clear, I admired the role President Bush played in helping America through 9/11. A lesser person may not have been up to the task. I believe that President Bush had his heart in the right place when it came to a lot of his policies. For all of his now infamous misspeaks and inarticulate "Bushisms," there was something genuine about the man, something not staged, something real. I also believe that many of the criticisms made of President Bush were related to America's epidemic of narcissism and were undeserved.

The President of the United States has to look good and be image-perfect to satisfy narcissists who judge their president by how well he serves the role of being their flawless avatar. Narcissists often possess a distorted sense of self (toward the perfection end of the continuum) and are sensitive to anything, including their avatar, that is, not as perfect as they imagine themselves to be. President Bush's gaffes, misuse of words and his folksy style were more than America's narcissists could tolerate. Number 43 made them look bad, and when your avatar looks bad it is intolerable to narcissists.

Many of President Bush's critics were motivated by a desire to engage in ideological warfare. In particular, Michael Moore's criticism of President Bush's character, as betrayed by his facial affect, after having learned from Andy Card that America was under attack on 9/11, was a cheap shot. Since when did Moore become an expert at deciphering non-verbal facial expressions? I've seen Moore display more troubling character flawed facial expressions while being questioned by Wolf Blitzer.

You may disagree with every criticism I have made of Conservatives, Republicans, President Bush and his advisors, but you can't reasonably disagree with the fact that President Bush and his policies served as the impetus for the election of President Obama. The Obama administration successfully used America's enmity toward President Bush and his policies for at least 6 years into his own administration to excuse the failures of his own policies. Exit polling conducted after the 2012 Presidential election found that a majority of voters still believed that President Bush was responsible for the sad state of America's economy despite the fact that President Obama had been in office for 4 years.

If you are bristling in response to my insistence that Conservatives apply personal responsibility to themselves, then you may not be up to the task of fighting AND winning the ideological war currently taking place in America. The fact is Conservatives, especially Republicans, have been outsmarted and outplayed by their Progressive adversaries. If you are defensive right now then you may need to think more about why Marxists have gotten as far as they have in taking over America, that is, if you want to win the battle for America's heart and soul.

It feels good to be dogmatic, literal and concrete, an ideologue. Ideologues on either end of the political continuum possess a self-righteousness that makes acquiring wisdom more difficult than it has to be. Traditional America was steeped in compassionate Conservatism, and no, I am not referencing the manipulative use of that term by some political operatives.

The psychological defect that beguiles Conservatives has been described as the tendency toward authoritarianism. This defect is what has made it possible for Marxists to effectuate their revolution in America. What follows is Adorno's (1950) description of this psychological state. I include this information here because it is my belief that authoritarianism is something to overcome. It is something to overcome for one's own personal development but must be overcome if statists are ever going to be kept from assuming totalitarian control. It is ironic, to say the least, that both statists and the authoritarians of the Right, are eerily similar in how they govern. Here is how Adorno described the authoritarian personality:

"Adorno, et al. (1950) viewed the authoritarian personality as having a strict superego that controls a weak ego unable to cope with strong id impulses. The resulting intrapsychic conflicts cause personal insecurities, resulting in that person's superego to adhere to externally imposed conventional norms (conventionalism), and to the authorities who impose these norms (authoritarian submission). The ego-defense mechanism of projection occurs as indicated when that person avoids self-reference of the anxiety producing id impulse, by displaying them onto "inferior" minority groups in the given culture (projectivity), with associated beliefs that are highly evaluative (power and toughness), and rigid (stereotypy). Additionally, there is a cynical view of mankind and a need for power and toughness resulting from the anxieties produced by perceived lapses in society's conventional norms (destructiveness and cynicism). Other characteristics of this personality type are a general tendency to focus upon those who violate conventional values and act harshly towards them (authoritarian aggression), a general opposition to subjective or imaginative tendencies (anti-intraception), a tendency to believe in mystic determination (superstition), and finally, an exaggerated concern with promiscuity."

I want to say a word about how to become a counter-revolutionary so that you don't become anxiety ridden, depressed, self-destructive and become like your adversary in the process. My training and experience informs me that some very nice and patriotic people collapse under the knowledge that a coordinated group of subversives are intent upon destroying the America our founders passed onto us. As an antidote to this malaise, I want to share with you the notion of The Happy Warrior.

Happy warriors don't all do the same thing. In the military an army is comprised of individuals, each with a specialty but working together as a unit. Not everyone gets or wants to "walk the point." Not every soldier is a trained medic or communication's expert. You generally have a platoon leader but every soldier must be responsible for what it is he or she does.

Some of you will be content just knowing what's up in the world. If this book has helped in that regard then great. If that is all you want to do or ever want to do that is fine. Most people have talents and skills that can be helpful to the counter-revolution. Some folks have graphics skills, others are writers, and others may be good librarians and record keepers. Some readers of this book will become recruiters. Some will become counter-agents while still others will become featured speakers. Lawyers who read this book may choose to help bring counter-revolutionary battles into court. There is tremendous joy to be had in knowing that you are part of a patriotic movement. Hopefully, most everyone who has read this book will no longer be an easy victim for those subverting the United States of America.

Camaraderie is a great morale booster. However, many counter-revolutionaries are not natural gadflies or particularly social. The late Groucho Marx was reportedly asked to attend a swanky dinner hosted by the Friars Club, an exclusive club for the elite of Hollywood. According to legend, Groucho sent a telegram to the Friars that read "Any club that would have me as a member I would not want to join." A lot of would-be counter-revolutionaries share Groucho's sentiment.

Knowing that others, like you, share a common awareness is a potent energy and morale booster. For those of you who are relatively young, you may not have had the pleasure and great benefit that comes from having a strong American identity. It was taken from you, actually stolen from you to be precise, by those who purposefully brainwashed you. Once you get that feeling of national pride back, I guarantee you that you will become even more upset with the social engineers who brainwashed you beginning in your early childhood.

The first thing Socialists will do with this book, if anything, is to ignore it. If Communists decide that they must address this book, then I anticipate that its contents will be gone over with a fine-toothed comb, looking for anything that can undermine it or its author. If Progressives made a big deal out of Mitt Romney's reference to "binders" full of women, then I can virtually guarantee you that they will find something to spin, misquote, take out of context or bastardize in service to their cause. That is what they do.

If Progressives decide that they must address this book it will not be because of its content, per se, and certainly not because of me, but because of its existential threat to their movement. This book may awaken Americans to the need to become peaceful counter-revolutionaries. If a viable counter-revolutionary force takes shape and becomes a formidable opponent to the collectivists currently running roughshod over America, then expect Marxists to retaliate.

What they have done in the past can be objectively described as ruthless and without regard to human decency. They can justify any act, no matter how heinous, because to them the end justifies the means. You must always keep this principle in mind: The America handed down to you is worth protecting and passing onto your children and grandchildren just as intended by our forefathers. We don't need change, we need to reconstitute our once great country that is under attack from people who hate it and want to first steal it then transform it into an abomination. Non-Americans, believe it or not, take great solace in thinking that if they had to escape from tyranny, they could escape to the United States. Don't allow that dream to be taken away because you failed to protect your country.

For those of you, and there are many, who hate rich people and corporate power, please consider that the antidote to the objects of your hatred and the abuses of capitalism is not Statism. Believe me when I tell you that embracing Statism as an antidote to corporate abuse and greed is like going from the proverbial frying pan into the fire.

Progressivism, when taken to its logical and inevitable end point, is tantamount to creating one big super-strain corporation. The government's corporation can't be sued, doesn't respond to market forces, has no competition and has plenary powers. This last point is critical to understand, especially for those who, like all reasonable men, despise abusive corporate power, greed and avarice. The worst corporation may lie, cheat, steal and exploit people, but it can't arrest you, search your home, put you in jail or put you to death, but the government corporation can.

So many corporate abuses can be mitigated if not eliminated by educating the public. Educating the public will become irrelevant when Statists set up their government-based corporation. When Progressives take control of

118

America they will set up a corporation that doesn't care if it runs out of money, it will just tax its customers. There are no anti-trust laws to keep a Progressive government/corporation in check. You can't boycott a government like you can a corporation. Progressive's government will have no competitors. It will become the ultimate monopoly. Yet, many Liberal activists are unwittingly helping to create a corporation that will be like taking the worst capitalist organization/corporation you can imagine and putting it on steroids.

Michael Moore may not care about any of my warnings because he has auditioned for and anticipates being given a job as one of the government's corporate officers. But if things don't work out, I promise you that Michael will not be editing close ups of a Progressive leader as part of a "hit piece" on Progressives as he did in Fahrenheit 9/11. History informs us that Michael will end up in Siberia if he even flirts with the idea of making a derisive documentary of the government's super-strain corporation.

A wise man once reminded me during a trying time that most things can be fixed and virtually anything can be made better. As a counter-revolutionary you will join some of the most principled people who have ever walked on Earth. From every bad thing comes something good. And just think, you may be God's reply to the subversives amongst us. Without those trying to ruin the country given to us, your meaning in life may not have been as great. When you do God's work you invoke all the protections and favor your creator gave to you. May God help YOU restore America.

INDEX

1820's 34
1950's 72, 91
1960's 19, 34, 72, 73, 105
911 ....5, 113, 119
Abortion 73
Accolades......................12, 13, 108
ACLU 94
Adultery....................................... 75
Affectation 107
Affective 102
Agnostic 4, 5
Alaska 84, 85
Aleksander Solzhenitsyn.......43, 44
America 2, i, ii, iii, 2, 3, 4, 5, 6, 7, 8,
    14, 17, 19, 20, 22, 25, 27, 32,
    33, 34, 36, 37, 38, 40, 41, 42,
    44, 45, 57, 58, 59, 60, 68, 71,
    72, 73, 74, 75, 77, 79, 81, 83,
    86, 89, 91, 92, 93, 94, 95, 96,
    97, 99, 101, 102, 103, 104, 105,
    106, 108, 109, 110, 111, 112,
    113, 114, 116, 117, 118, 119
    American exceptionalism 22,
        105
        American flag 25
        American patriots............40, 75
        American values 3, 17
        Americana 19, 26, 111
Anglo-Christians 2, 6, 25
    Anglo Christian Truths......... 25
    Anglo-European Christians 4
Anxiety..............................41, 116
Apology...................................... 26
Atheist..........................4, 5, 94, 98
Atlanta Journal Constitution 85
Avarice 111, 112, 118
Bezmenov, Yuri.......iii, 43, 97, 103
Biblical.. 2
Biden, Joe 51, 52
Big Foot 69
Bill of Rights 2
Black 33, 34, 35, 36, 42
    Black Christian 33
    Black Conservative 35
    Black Nuclear Family........... 36
    Black Stereotype.................. 36

Blitzer, Wolf 49, 50, 114
Borders ....i, 17
Brainwashing..33, 77, 90, 104, 109,
    117
Cable....................................63, 83
Camaraderie 116
Capitalist 112
Capitalists................................. 112
Carnal desire.............................. 7
Children....i, 3, 6, 8, 11, 12, 13, 14,
    15, 19, 21, 22, 25, 29, 30, 32,
    33, 34, 36, 42, 44, 54, 60, 62,
    64, 71, 72, 73, 104, 107, 111,
    118
    Christian Children 22
Christmas......................20, 25, 105
Church of England 6
Civil rights movement............... 34
Class warfare 12, 64
Clique 68, 108
CNN 49, 53, 83, 97
Collective mind......................... 41
Collectivists 1, 108
Comedy sketch 26, 49, 50
Communism.................55, 99, 101
    Communist...24, 77, 78, 79, 83,
        91, 93, 94, 96, 97, 98, 99,
        101, 105, 106, 107, 110
    Communist Party............... 105
    Communist Party USA....... 105
    Communist revolutionaries .. 24
    Communist sympathizers 78,
        79, 97, 99, 107
Complainer.........77, 78, 81, 82
Comrade ..1, 34, 35, 43, 51, 53, 54,
    55, 56, 57, 58, 59, 60, 70, 72,
    73
Condescending 48, 50, 52, 84
Condom.................................... 32
Confiscation ....i, 15, 43, 99
Conservative.......31, 38, 63, 72, 73,
    110, 111, 112, 114
Conspiracy 25, 61, 91, 98, 99
Constitution 2, 85
Counter-revolutionary:...23, 77, 79,
    83, 90, 91, 97, 116, 117, 119

120

Couric, Katie 50, 51, 83, 85, 86, 87, 88, 89
Cowards 67
Critic 77
Culture ... 6, 8, 9, 11, 14, 17, 18, 19, 21, 22, 23, 30, 33, 35, 36, 37, 38, 60, 63, 71, 72, 73, 81, 108
Cute 48
Declaration of Independence 2
Delusion 21
Demographics........................i, 73
Détournement 76
Digital media............................ 36
Dismissiveness ... 46, 47, 49, 51, 52, 53, 82, 88
Displacement of responsibility... 42
Distortion.................................. 9
Divorce 29
Dole... 28
Dragon..................................... 94
Drama.... 35, 46, 50, 51, 52, 54, 63, 69, 80, 88, 112, 113
Drugs ....i, 40, 41, 42, 59
Elites ....i, 66, 107
Enemy i, iii, 2, 3, 4, 5, 6, 7, 8, 9, 10, 11, 12, 13, 15, 17, 18, 19, 20, 21, 22, 23, 24, 25, 27, 28, 29, 30, 31, 32, 33, 36, 38, 40, 41, 42, 44, 45, 48, 52, 53, 55, 56, 59, 66, 68, 70, 71, 73, 74, 78, 82, 110
English 19, 92
Entitlement .. 13, 33, 34, 43, 70, 80, 102, 111, 113
Entrepreneurship..................28, 42
Envy ....i, 13, 15, 35, 70
Epithet 35
Equal...........................9, 10, 18, 19
Equilibrium............................i, 9
ER physicians............................ 86
Erlich, Paul 73
Evangelical 61
Evans, M. Stanton............. 102, 103
Evilness..................................... 35
Exceptional 13, 23
Exceptionalism 22, 105
Fatherhood 73, 74
Feelings 15, 32, 41, 70, 71
Female..................................22, 30

Fire..............................24, 83, 118
Flat affect.......................48, 51, 82
FNC 83
Forward.......................1, 45, 106
Fracturing................................. 33
Free love 32
Freedom 6, 44, 95, 106
    Freedom of religion............... 6
Genuflection 26
Germ warfare 71
Gibson, Charlie.. 47, 48, 49, 50, 83, 84
God.....4, 7, 11, 23, 61, 75, 95, 119
    God fearing........................ 61
    God is myth........................ 23
    God-given talent 11
Grandparents............................ 36
Granny glasses 84
Greed......28, 74, 75, 110, 112, 118
Groucho Marx 116
Guilt........13, 31, 32, 34, 58, 68, 70
Gulag Archipelago 43
Gun Control ....i, 43
guns
    gun control ....i, 43
Guns 44, 45, 59, 60, 63
    Gun control 44
Hagel...............................100, 101
Hagel, Chuck 99, 100, 101
Happy Holidays........................ 25
Haves 15
Hedonism 15, 29, 31, 42, 98
High school cheerleader............ 85
Hispanic................................... 42
Hitler, Adolf 53, 81, 82
Hollywood 63, 67, 69
Homicide 107
Homophobe 61
Homosexuality.......................... 75
Huffington Post........................ 95
Ideology.... 22, 23, 87, 98, 101, 105, 109, 111
Immigration 18, 73
    Anti-immigrant 18
    Illegal immigration............... 18
    Immigrants 17, 18, 71, 73
    Un-assimilating, immigrants . 73
Immoral.................................. 108
Inconceivable ....i, 37, 38, 39

121

Injustice.....iii, 9, 10, 27, 36, 69, 75, 105

Inner-city....................................42

Insensitive 24, 25

Intolerance.....9, 18, 21, 22, 23, 61, 108

iPad..97

Islam 4, 5, 6, 22, 88, 89

Izvestia ....i, 83, 92

Jealousy................i, 15, 35, 70, 108

Jesus..75

John King...................................49

KGB ....iv, 97

King, John..................................49

Kings...................16, 67, 69, 75

Language....................................19

Latin America 73

Leningrad...................................43

Lerma, Xavier.......................92, 96

Libertines................................i, 31

Macro-cultural......................71, 72

Male 22, 74

Manifesto 72, 73, 93

Mantra 18, 32, 34, 57, 70, 111

Marginalize 62, 77, 78

Marijuana...................................41

Marxism............2, 78, 91, 106, 109

Marx....................................116

Marxist1, 24, 77, 79, 82, 83, 90, 91, 97, 101, 106, 110, 111

Mass media-entertainment complex...............................104

McCarthyism 58, 91, 96, 97, 100

McCarthy58, 91, 100, 101, 102, 103

Media-entertainment complex.....7, 32, 56, 81, 86, 88, 89, 97, 101, 107

Meg Ryan..............................83, 85

Melting pot................................71

Men..31, 32, 36, 59, 68, 70, 73, 74, 90, 111, 118

Merit 11, 13, 18, 36, 62

Merry Christmas.................25, 105

Metaphor 90

Military...25, 44, 59, 62, 79, 80, 93, 105, 116

Militia....................................44, 79

Millennium ....i, 19

Mind-altering substances............32

Misanthropy..............................75

Misquote 117

Miss American Pie................92, 95

Moral relativism.....................7, 15

Morality.........................7, 15, 57

Mosque 5

Motive............................102, 106

MSNBC..............30, 100, 101, 102

Multiculturalism.......i, 6, 19, 63, 81

Muslims 5, 22, 88, 89

Narcissism........................73, 113

Narcissists 113

National Anthem 20

National Rifleman.....................85

Nazis 53

Network 61, 82, 97

Non-assimilating immigrants.17, 18

Non-threatening disguise 106

Non-traditional..........................29

Non-verbal communication.46, 47, 50, 87

Nuclear family..3, 4, 29, 30, 31, 32, 73

Obama, Barack..53, 82, 88, 92, 93, 94, 114

Occupy Wall Street 70, 80

OCD...42

Operations manualii, iii, 57, 66, 69, 74, 83, 109

Operations Manual.....................iii

Operative43, 50, 53, 54, 81, 82, 89, 97

Palin, Sarah..47, 48, 49, 50, 51, 82, 83, 84, 85, 88, 97, 107

Parents7, 22, 29, 30, 32, 64, 72, 74, 104

Passive.......................................98

Patriotism...................................20

Payoffs.......................................28

Payouts......................................28

Perma-victims 36

Pilgrims 71, 105

Pimps 36

Platoon leader..........................116

Pledge of 20, 72, 104

Political Class 75

Political correctness 91

Postural alignment 48

Pregnancy.................................. 31
Producer 82
Progressivism .1, 24, 55, 78, 80, 86, 97, 98, 99, 102, 104, 106, 107, 110, 111, 112, 117, 118, 119
Prolonged Adolescence 74
Prostitutes 109
Psychology 63, 110
  Psychiatrist............................ 70
  Psychological ..6, 36, 40, 51, 52, 53, 69, 72, 74, 75, 79, 84, 101, 102, 105, 107, 109, 112
  Psychological warfare40, 51, 53, 69, 72, 74, 84, 101, 102, 105, 109
  Psychotropic medication 42
  Psychotropic medications..... 42
Public school..2, 3, 6, 8, 15, 44, 64, 70, 72, 104, 105, 106
  Public school teachers 106
Purge...................................59, 62
Queen.............................16, 67, 69
Racism 34
Redistribution 15, 71, 99
Regressive 1
Religion....4, 5, 6, 8, 17, 20, 21, 29, 32, 62, 63, 109
  Religion of Tolerance............. 5
Roesgen 53, 54
Romney, Mitt............................117
Ryan, Paul.............................51, 52
Satan 95
Saturday Night Live 50
Scandal...................................... 75
scowling................................48, 51
Seething subclass....................... 42
Self-destruct 25, 29
Selfishness................................. 28
Semantic legerdemain................ 67
Senator...58, 91, 99, 100, 101, 102, 103
  Senator Joe McCarthy 102
  Senator Ted Cruz........100, 101
Sex 30, 31, 32, 59, 62, 64, 108
  Sex without obligation 31
Sexual......20, 32, 36, 58, 72, 74, 75
  Sexual abuse 75
  Sexual mores 20
Sin 107

Skeptical.........................21, 51, 53
Skullduggery 83
Slavery....................i, 33, 34, 35, 36
Social.2, iii, 8, 9, 10, 11, 16, 32, 40, 55, 67, 68, 69, 73, 75, 77, 91, 98, 105, 116, 117
  Social engineering..8, 16, 68, 91
  Social gadflies 67
  Social justice 32, 40, 55, 91
  Social media 2, 77
Socialism................................... 79
  Socialists ......i, 1, 79, 91, 97, 98, 102, 117
Solzhenitsyn 43, 44
South...............................34, 44, 80
Soviet Union 73, 92, 94, 95
Stalin, Joseph 44, 58, 93
Stealth mode 91
Stigmatized...25, 35, 91, 96, 97, 98, 101, 102, 111
  Stigmatized label.35, 91, 96, 97, 101, 102, 111
Strategy...48, 51, 57, 67, 92, 96, 97, 106
Stupid.....23, 38, 46, 51, 53, 64, 68, 75, 79, 81, 100
Substances................................. 42
Suburbs..................................... 42
Subversion ....ii, 41, 78, 106
  Subversives .90, 91, 96, 98, 106, 107, 108, 109, 110, 116, 119
  Subvert ...29, 38, 52, 59, 66, 68, 77, 109
Superiority ..46, 47, 48, 49, 51, 107
Symbolic 46, 51, 70
  Symbolic gestures 70
  Symbolic outrage 46, 51
Tabula Rasa ....i, 11
Tactics.................................... 101
Take out of context................. 117
talent 11, 12, 33
TEA Party................................. 80
Tele-evangelists 75
The Happy Warrior 116
The Progressive Virus...91, 99, 110
Theo-political ideology 22
Tobacco 41
Tolerance i, 5, 6, 21, 22, 23, 29, 32, 40, 55, 57, 107

Tolerance solution 21
Toxic.. 33
Traditional America ..3, 17, 40, 42, 44, 73, 74, 111, 114
Traitor....................................iii, 43
Treason...............................38, 59
TV...62, 63
U.S. Citizen............................... 17
Uncle Tom 35
Unfair..................................14, 24
United Socialist States of America ....ii, 95
Useful idiots...........57, 63, 108, 109
USSR ....i, 6, 43, 56, 57, 83, 91, 92, 103
Verboten.............................i, 24, 90
Village ....i, 8, 29, 30, 81

Virus 23, 60
Washington Times 85
Welfare state.......................28, 111
White House 91, 95, 97
Whites.. 33
White Guilt 34
whores.. 36
Wintour, Anna 107, 108
Wisconsin 91
Witch Hunt 100, 101
Wizard of Oz.........................62, 90
Women..22, 31, 32, 36, 68, 70, 73, 90, 108, 117
World Trade Center Towers 5
Worry...........41, 42, 59, 63, 64, 83
Zero Population Growth 73

CPSIA information can be obtained
at www.ICGtesting.com
Printed in the USA
BVHW041917040620
580930BV00014B/517

9 781621 373049